MYLAPORE TO MASSACHUSETTS

notionpress
.com

MYLAPORE
TO
MASSACHUSETTS

R. DHAMODHARAN

notionpress.com

Notion Press

Old No. 38, New No. 6
McNichols Road, Chetpet
Chennai - 600 031

First Published by Notion Press 2016

ISBN 978-93-5206-731-2

Dedication

This book "Mylapore to Massachusetts" is dedicated
to the memory of my parents Ubhayavedanthi Kaduvankudi
Raghavachariar Swamy and
Kaadaanthethi Renganayaki Ammal

Contents

Preface

I was raised in Mylapore and later in Nanganallur, the cultural hubs of Chennai, with traditional cultural values. My orthodox and religious mother, hardworking, honest and affectionate father and doting paternal grandmother shaped my life. My early values and beliefs were also shaped by the social surrounding consisting of fisher folks, poor, lower middle class, middle class, in that order. Those were the days when the radio and cinema were the only ways to reach out to the public. A time when test cricket was much loved and considered the ultimate measure of a cricketer's ability… The television was still unknown and the landline telephone was a luxury only the rich, privileged and powerful sections of society could afford… Electricity was at its infancy and the best known utility of electricity was lighting the darkness through the yellow glow of the Edison's lamp unless of course one was rich, in which case a fan or two would help in beating the heat of the day!

My daily life revolved around going to the temples, recitation of slokams or prayer at home, a strict lactovegetarian diet and strict observations of rules framed by my mother. Early on, I developed natural sympathy to economically and socially under- privileged people who had to fight existential challenges on a daily basis, similar to mine. Our day to day life had a lot to do with the actual functioning of the government that provided: a meager monthly salary of my father, dry food and kerosene fuel in the ration shop, train and bus transportation, education and health care in government schools and health centres. This provided me an opportunity to observe, listen and learn alternate ways of thinking and living on all fronts through interactions at school, playground, temple and other places outside my home.

My early life left me with some "fixed" value system that came out of observations such as: separate high schools for boys and girls, a man and a woman coming together only in marriage, arranged marriages, no visible exhibition of physical "intimacy" between grown men and women in public, respect for elders, totally unarmed policeman, literally no visible exhibition of affluence but religious leanings, very few privately owned motor vehicles, display of political affiliations in the form of writings and drawings on walls, printed wall-posters here-there-and-everywhere, people who could be disturbed at will in public places for an enquiry with regard to address and availability of facilities, street side shops (Potti Kadai) that stocked small eatables, biscuits, fruits, newspapers and magazines, mobile fruits and vegetables vendors, free intermixing of people with cows, buffaloes, dogs, chicken, pigs and donkeys on the street and so on… In short, the life that was I exposed to was full of an unpredictable mixture of certainty and uncertainty, in time. This randomness was an accepted way of life, may it be supply of electricity, drinking water and essentials in ration shops, punctuality of bus and train services, conditions of road, availability of telephone lines as well as accessing the right person with the right number!

With the above socio-cultural-economic background and without any preparation that my friends-to-be had, such as watching Western and Indian movies, reading Western/

Indian novels, exchanging information through friends and relatives, I landed up in the USA for my higher education. This shocked and rattled me to no extent during the initial stages. It started with the first observation of the gigantic infrastructure and orderly functioning in the form of J.F. Kennedy International Airport at New York upon landing in the USA. This was immediately followed by the "get lost" response that I received from an old person to whom I approached for help to locate the nearest public telephone booth. My sin was that I disturbed him while he was busy "making-out" with a young girl who would qualify to be his granddaughter in my perspective! This was soon followed by a series of shocks in the cultural frontier. As any living being, I got used to the American way of life, which took about one year. In this process, I learnt a lot about my society, the American society and myself. Whatever I had learnt during my initial stage of life was not absolute and when taken out of context made absolutely no sense on any grounds. There was only one universal value "thou shall not hurt the others". Good and bad people are part of both the societies and the American society was not very different from ours if one were to look from the right perspective.

As much as I could come to terms with different belief and value systems and adjust and accept the American values, I had great difficulty adopting or living by it. The work environment in the USA was just perfect and there were plenty of opportunities for my wife who had earned a Ph.D. in Molecular and Cell Biology at the University of Massachusetts with the additional possibility of our children not being restricted and limited to opportunities of growth if we choose to continue to live in the USA. But at the home and social front, I really missed the gay and colour of Mylapore. There was a deep desire to protect our strong cultural identity and pass it on to the next generation as the American "melting-pot" would engulf all of our past and accommodate it the way the English language had done to Tamil terms such as "Mangaai" (to Mango), "Catamaram" to "Catamaran" and so on. To preserve the vintages of the past, it was essential that I lived in the home-ambience with my family and adopt to changes that were taking place in the home front. This mental battle between my first 23 years of life, programmed and shaped in Mylapore/ Nanganallur, and the new way of life that I got accustomed to in Massachusetts during the next 10 years drove me to the point where it appeared that it was more suitable for us and our family to take home the lessons learnt from the USA and use the skills and experiences gained living in the US to contribute towards changes in my society. I really wanted the Mylapore way of life and could not accept the American way of life for my children.

In this book, I share my personal experiences of going from Mylapore to Massachusetts via Nanganallur with the fond sense of recalling what was nostalgic about the Mylapore/Nanganallur way of life and what appeared unusual about the Massachusetts ways of life from a pre-conditioned Mylaporean way of life. I think that each way of life, in its DNA, has some stored memory of lessons from the past that was relevant to that past and possibly the immediate future. This is being passed on from generation to generation under the assumption that the past is likely to continue into the future. I write this book with the fond hope of sharing my lesson that "nothing is really more valuable or less valuable unless the context, time and place are defined precisely".

This semi-fiction aim is to bring out the perspective of one of the "viewers" as the "view" happens and does not aim to influence the image and character of people, groups and Institutions, with which I was closely associated with great pride all my life, in any way. I have changed names to protect the privacy of people.

Acknowledgements

The author thanks his wife Dr. Rama Dhamodharan and children Rishy and Nappinnai. The author also thanks his brothers (Narayanan, Madhavan, Mukundan and Anand) and sisters (Pushpavalli, Amirthavalli, Saroja and Hemamalini) and grandmother Rukmini Ammal for sharing all the testing times. Special thanks to my dear friend Late Prof. Dillip Veeraraghavan who was a pillar of support during the initial period of returning back home when the "heat" of reverse-cultural shock was on.

Mylapore... Values Imprinted

Ramu was born in Nagapattinam, a small town in old Thanjavur (modern day Tiruvarur) district of Tamil Nadu. He was the seventh child of Kannan and Komala. His mother gave birth to him at the house of her parents, Kaadanthethi Aravamudha Iyengar, a teacher at National School, Nagapattinam, and Paruthicheri Sundaram Iyengar Komalavalli. In those days, small towns did not have any hospitals, not even a primary health centre. Even important issues of birth, death, and maternal health were left to faith and fate.

Soon after Ramu's birth, Kannan moved into a government-owned flat meant for lower income groups (LIG) in Foreshore Estate, Mylapore. It was called Pattinnappakkam in Tamil and was hardly 500 metres away from the Bay of Bengal coast. First generation migrants from villages inhabited Foreshore Estate with the dreams of blooming along with the growing city of Madras (now known as Chennai). In those days electrical power and the Edison's lamp was the best technology they had been exposed to and afford and power shortage was more the norm than an exception. At Foreshore Estate, only the rich and powerful, who were fewer in number, could afford electricity operated fans. But with the sea breeze setting in as early as 11 a.m, there was hardly any need for a fan or an air-conditioner those days.

On the eastern side of Foreshore Estate, about 250 metres away from the coast, there were a number of apartments meant for the fisher-folk. The state government's Slum Development Board built them so that seafarers had a proper home to live in. A number of middle-income group (MIG) flats were also built by the state government on the southern and southwestern side of Foreshore Estate, flanked by the Santhome High Road on the west. A prominent landmark on this road was Hotel Romus.

There was a primary health centre and an elementary school in Foreshore Estate, besides a public distribution centre, more commonly known as a ration shop. The ration shop sold items such as kerosene, rice and sugar, in limited quantities, at subsidized rates. There was also a community hall in Foreshore Estate, where functions such as weddings and birthdays were held. The annual Ayyapan Poojai also took place here. Once in five years, the community hall also served as a polling centre for the state and central elections. The northern and southern parts of Foreshore Estate were home to ministers in the state government and judges. These areas also housed private bungalows owned by the rich.

The Madras Music College and the Adyar River were located on the southwestern side of Foreshore Estate. The southeastern region housed fisher-folks at the Slum Development Board flats. This area was popularly called Nochikkuppam. Any child growing up in Foreshore Estate was exposed to the socio-economic and religious values and practices of the poor, middle class and the rich alike.

Ramu had his early education at the Foreshore Estate Elementary School. His teachers had a lasting influence on the way Ramu looked at life. One such teacher was nicknamed *gundu* teacher due to her girth. She was strict yet affectionate. She lived in the fisher-folks' area along with her relatives and husband who was called Iyer. At school and at the end of every academic year, the teachers often discussed the final year SSLC (Secondary School Leaving Certificate) examination papers. Whenever they were stumped by certain questions, it was Ramu who came up with the right answers. *Gundu* teacher was pleasantly surprised by Ramu's extraordinary ability. On quizzing him, she found out that Ramu paid close attention to his elder brother whenever he studied aloud. The teacher realised that Ramu had a phenomenal memory. She wanted to tap this and ensure that his naughty behaviour didn't come in the way of his studies in future. So she met Ramu's mother regularly with updates on his progress at school.

Once Ramu brought home his monthly report card and showed it to his mother. He had scored 99 in all subjects and 100 in Mathematics. Ramu usually scored 100 in all subjects. He always stood first in class. On seeing his progress report, Ramu's mother chided him.

Ramu's mother: What happened to that one mark in the other subjects?

Ramu: It is the teacher's mistake in English.

"Why should the teacher make a mistake? And what about the other subjects?"

"I made a silly mistake in Geography."

"Why?" She gives a few whacks. "If you do not score 100 in the upcoming tests, do not come home and do not show your report card to me."

His mother's strict expectations left a deep impact on Ramu. She was always driving him to do better.

Ramu's childhood days in Mylapore were happy and fun-filled. He and his friends collected the aluminium flaps on glass bottles used to sell milk, which were used as mock currency. They also played 'tennis-ball' cricket and traditional games such as *goli* and *gilli thanda*. The children from the middle-income groups played cricket with better bats and balls. They also played a game called trade, which revolved around the business of buying and selling. The rich children played tennis and cricket. They also played with battery-operated toy scooters and cars. Ramu played with used cycle tyres, especially during the weekends, jogging beside them as they were pushed by his hand held stick to roll slowly. He also played cricket with a tennis ball, because not everyone could afford a real cricket ball. Besides playing, Ramu loved listening to cricket commentary on the radio. Even as he had fun, he ensured his academic performance met his mother's expectations.

Ramu and his cycle tyre could be regularly spotted on the streets where Seerkazhi Govindarajan, a popular and gifted singer, and M. S. Viswanathan, a well-known Tamil film music director, resided. Their houses had trees with juicy mangoes, guava and big *nellikai* (gooseberry). Ramu often aimed a few small stones at them and on quite a few lucky occasions, he managed to get away with fruits, without getting caught. Whenever Ramu got tired of his neigbourhood, he took a trip to the old Adyar river bridge with his cycle tyre. This locality was home to several high court judges and ministers. Like dogs marking out their territory, Ramu and his friends went around their neighbourhood with cycle tyres, mapping out the territory, checking out new developments, and visiting a friend or two. The Foreshore Estate area had quite a few important places to hang out.

One such haunt was the bus terminus on routes 12-B (Vadapalani to Foreshore Estate), 12-C (T. Nagar to Foreshore Estate, later extended to K. K. Nagar to Fore Shore Estate) and 27-D (Integral Coach Factory to Foreshore Estate). The terminus was located on Santhome Main Road adjacent to Hotel Romus and Sea Lord. The senior boys gathered at the bus terminus and discussed the India-West Indies and the India-England cricket series, over a cup of coffee or tea. After the heated discussion, the boys invariably hit the beach at night, which was about 500 metres away. There they listened to BBC (British Broadcasting Corporation) radio's cricket commentary. This was their routine practice till the match ended that day in West Indies or England. Hanging out in the beach was an essential part of their day's activities. The radio reception at home was often weak and no passionate lover of the game could wait till the next day to know the score from the newspapers. The beach session with a transistor was a do-or-die situation for the big boys.

During the first ten years of his life, Ramu often fell sick with sore throat and cold. Each time, his mother took him to the Primary Health Centre where the doctor prescribed a 'teramycin/sulfamycin' antibiotic injection. If this did not cure the problem, she took him to Dr. Athmalingam, a private medical practitioner, on Appu Mudali Street. During these doctor visits, it was Ramu's mother or his sister Kumudha who carried Ramu on their hips. On the way to the doctor's clinic, Ramu's religious and god-fearing mother made sure they stopped by at the Karumariamman temple, located directly across from the house of the famous Tamil film music director M. S. Viswanathan, to pray for a fast recovery. The temple poosari gave them sacred white ash, which was smeared generously on Ramu's forehead. Dr. Athmalingam, a general physician, was a very kind man. His pharmacist, Sathyamurthy, too was very caring and compassionate. He knew Ramu's father well and took extra efforts in helping his family members. Ramu was a regular at Dr. Athmalingam's clinic. He was in his clinic at least once a month, either for sore throat, fever or an injury sustained during play. Ramu often got hurt while playing. He had been to the doctor's clinic for cuts on his eyebrows, forehead, knee and foot. He had quite a few stitches on his body, besides losing a few of his front teeth when he tried to demonstrate his prowess to his cousins. He was always reckless and often lost control of himself while playing. As a result, Ramu's father had to spend more time with him than with his other children.

When Ramu completed class five, he was forced to give up evening play. In fact, even when he was just in class four, Sanskrit classes at Sankara Mutt, in the heart of Mylapore, replaced evening play during the weekdays. The Sanskrit teacher came all the way from a place called Ambattur, on the outskirts of Madras, in a bus. In those days, one had to start well in advance (perhaps in the afternoon itself) from Ambattur to reach Mylapore in the evening.

The teacher, who had a gifted voice, would start the class with the rendering of one of Adi Sankara's verse.

"Mudakaraatha Modakam, Sada Vimukthi Sadhakaam

Kaladaravathamsakam Vilasi Lokha Rakshakam

Anaayyakaikka Nayaakam Vinashitheba Dhythyakam

Natha Shubhashu Naashakkam Namamitham Vinayakkam"

The meaning of the above Sanskrit verse goes thus:

"I worship Lord Ganesha (Vinayakam) who holds the *modakam* (a sweet eat) in hand. He bestows upon us salvation. He who wears the moon as an ornament or a crown in his head, he is the sole protector and the leader of the leaderless. He who destroyed the elephant demon Gajasura, he quickly erases the sins of those who prostrate before him."

Ramu's Sanskrit teacher insisted on reciting by rote every verse. So much that, Ramu, even 47 years later, still remembered the *slokam* with which his Sanskrit class ended.

"Raamo Raajamanihi Sada Vijayate, Raamam Ramesham Bhaje, Raamena-Abhihatha Nishaacara-Camuuhu Raamaya Tasmai Namaha,

Ramaan Naasti Paraayanam Parataram Raamasya Dasoosmyaham, Raamo Chitalyas-Sada Bhavathu may bho Raama Maamudhara"

"Rama, the jewel among kings is always Victorious. Revere the lord of Sita.

By Rama is destroyed, the Army of the Demons. I salute that Rama.

Such equivalence to Rama does not exist. Last and supreme refuge, of whom I am a servant.

In Rama mind lies absorbed. Oh that Rama, grant me salvation."

This verse teaches the Rama Shabdham of the Akarantha Pulinkaha Rama Sabhtaha grammar, which is special to Sanskrit grammar. Rama, the person, gets addressed as Raamo, Rammam, Raamena, Raamaya, Raaman, Raamasya, Raamo and Raama ('by Rama,' 'to Rama,' 'that Rama') depending on the association of Rama with some specific action.

On the southern side of Foreshore Estate were the backwaters, a cemetery, and the Madras music college. The spotlessly clean cemetery, with perfectly symmetrical headstones and tombstones, was used to bury Englishmen and women. During the cycle tyre trips to Nochikuppam and the Adyar River, the boys sometimes spotted 'foreigners' on the beach, nearly naked. According to the boys, only those with exceptionally pink skin were 'foreigners.' The boys who managed to spot the 'foreigners' first immediately conveyed this piece of news to the rest of their squad. They talked about it so animatedly as though they were the first ones to scale Mount Everest. Ramu and his friends were curious to see if the 'foreigners' had any extra parts in their body that distinguished them from the locals. The curious glances of the boys irritated the 'foreigners.' They would scream and threaten the boys. Even as they moved to another part of the beach, the boys' squad hunted them down again. But the boys didn't dare venture beyond Nochikuppam and the Adyar River for fear of trespassing into unfamiliar territory.

Festivals marked the calendar of Mylapore. It started with the *Maarkazhi* month (January) '*bhajanais*' (musical praise of the Lord accompanied by supporting instruments) in which men in the neighbourhood used to go through the '*maada veethis*' or streets around the temple, during the early morning hours, singing the praise of the good lord. This meant that the children had to get up at wee hours of 4 to 5 a.m. and step into the street steeped in dew to seek the blessings of the elders who were doing the rounds. At the end of January, it was the *St. Lazarus* festival time. During this the devotees pull festival massively decorated chariots through the streets. The most attractive aspect of this festival for the children was that street hawkers displayed a variety of toys and goodies on either side of the street and one could enjoy the merry-go-around during this time along with a variety of "*mittaais*" or sweets tied around one's wrist in the form of a band. This is followed by the annual exams and from the month of *Panguni* (middle of March to middle of April) the *Brahmotsavam* or Annual Festival of the Kapaleeswarar temple starts. During this time, Mylapore really gets into a celebrating mood as it is summer holidays time for children. The '*Arupathimoovar*' festival is the height of this celebration when the idols of sixty-three '*Nayanmaars*,' the ardent blessed devotees of Lord Siva, are taken in palanquin through the streets of Mylapore. The folks in Myalpore take pride in quenching the thirst of the visitors with buttermilk that is given for free. During the festival of Navaratri, celebrated across ten days in September/ October every year, the boys' crew visited several houses in Foreshore Estate, Mandavelipakkam and Mylapore, even if they did not know anyone in the household. The boys looked forward to seeing the *kolu* (an elaborate arrangement of dolls on steps) and, of course, devouring the free *sundal* (protein-rich boiled lentils) given to visitors. So a visit every

evening to a few houses took care of the boys' dinner. Every household made different kinds of *sundal* each day; it was like a test of their culinary and presentation skills with the boys commenting and rating the *sundal* prepared in each house. The last festival for the year was the *Ayyappa Poojai* or the worship conducted by devotees planning to visit Lord Ayyappa at Sabarimalai in the month of *Kartikai* (middle of November to middle of December). This was the time when the community hall in Foreshore Estate was used to feed the poor. The most attractive feature of this festival for children was that an elephant would be present during the entire festival season and it was some sight to watch the quantity of food taken by it.

Ramu and his siblings were given rigorous religious training and had to recite Sanskrit verses twice a day. The children would not get their meal till they recited all the *slokams*. The older children did not get their dinner until they recited the *Vishnu Sahasranam*. Fasting on *Ekaadasi* and *Vaikunta Ekaadasi* was observed strictly. At home, everyone had his or her chores cut out. They had to wash the dirty dishes and clothes every day. Every day visits to the Srinivasa Perumal, Kesava Perumal and Kapaaleeswarar temples during the summer holidays were mandatory. Ramu's mother ensured that all her children visited the Vedanta Desikar *sannidhi* (the temple's sanctum sanctorum) and Kesava Perumal *sannidhi* in Mylapore once in the morning and once in the evening. They also had to go around the Hanuman *sannidhi* 16, 32, 64 or 108 times. Ramu's mother had a way of knowing if her children obeyed her or not. Ammaavasya Tharpanam or Ancestors Day was observed once a month on 'no-moon' days to remember three generation of ancestors. On those days, school started late after 10.30 a.m so that teachers could pay respects to their ancestors with the symbolic offering of black seeds and water. Weddings and death ceremonies were also elaborate affairs in his family.

Ramu grew up not only observing the social practices of Brahmin households, but he was also exposed to the customs of the fisher-folk in his neighbourhood. In fact, the fisher-folks influenced Ramu's social identity to a good extent and taught him a different perspective of life. Weddings in the fishermen's households were incomplete without film music, duly amplified over the public address system so that the entire community can get into the happy mood besides passing on the information that something happy was taking place. Even till date, Ramu remembered the film songs that were belted out during the social events.

"Vaarayo thozhi vaarayo, manapandal kaana vaarayo…" (Invitation to the girlfriend to the marriage hall by the bride.)

"Kalyana panthalile oru pen paarkkum neram ithu…" (The bride and groom's betrothal in the presence of relatives and friends.)

"Ponna pirantha aambalakita kazhuthaneetikanum, Avan onnu rendu moonu mudichu pota mattikkanum…"; (If you are born a woman, you have to extend your neck to the man so that he will make you his by tying three knots.)

"Antha mappillai kaathalithan, en kaaiyapudithan…" (The bridegroom loves me and holds me by my hand.)

"Thirumanamam thirumanamam theruvengum urvalamaam…" (The whole town is in a festive mood celebrating this marriage.)

"Mangalyam tantuna nena mamajeevana hetuna kanthe badhnami subhage twam jeeva saradasatam..." (This Sanskrit *slokam* means thus: May you, who is offering your neck to the man for tying the three knots, live one hundred years and let the man be blessed by the power of your holy knot.)

"Manamagale Marumagale Vaa Vaa!..." (Welcome to the daughter-in-law.)

"Indru vantha intha mayakkam ennai engengo kondupoguthu amma..."

(The intoxicated feeling I have today is taking me places.)

"Akkaluku valaikappu aththan mugathile pun siriupu, thanthane thanathane,..." (Today is sister's baby shower and brother-in-law is all smiles.)

"Kaathu kuduthu ketten, kuva kuva satham...".

(I listened carefully with my ears and I could hear the cries of the baby.)

The songs had such catchy tunes that Ramu was often found singing them at home, much to the chagrin of his mother who spanked him for singing "bad" songs.

Only when he grew up to be an adult did Ramu understand the explicit content of these songs. The lyrics, suggestive of the purpose of marriage, physical intimacy between man and woman, were simply unacceptable in a Brahmin household, causing elders to wince in discomfort.

If weddings were a cause of great celebration among the fisher-folk, so was death, which was regarded a happy farewell from this world. In total contrast to his community where death was a solemn, sordid event...

The final goodbye involved a procession in a decked-up wheel cart, from the dead person's home to the burial ground. The dead was dressed up well, replete with sunglasses, as though he or she was royalty. A few of the relatives and neighbours danced in front of the moving cart. Drums were played vigorously, accompanied by the blowing of the conch and the gong. Rose petals were strewn on the streets along the procession route.

At least a few people in the procession appeared to be in an inebriated state, perhaps in an attempt to downplay the grief that followed death. Some even poured kerosene inside their mouths and lit an open-flame with cotton wrapped on a metal or wooden rod.

Because of this strong influence from childhood, Ramu associated the fragrance of roses with death. Even to this day, the smell of roses as well as its presence on the streets evokes the deep sense of mortality of people in him. Although Ramu's parents kept him and the other children away from aspects of death and death-related ceremonies within their family, they could not hide them from the reality of the world around them. As a child, Ramu had sleepless nights after seeing a dead body on the palanquin. He often dreamt of the dead person waking up and speaking to him.

Holidays meant visiting relatives in Chennai with his father on his cycle. Every Aavani Avittam day, which falls in August-September, when the old sacred thread (Brahminical) is replaced by a new one, Ramu's father visited his sister, his uncle's son and his mother's sisters who lived in Triplicane, near the Parthasarathi Swami Temple. This day was special as Ramu was allowed to wear a fake thread. This is worn by boys (on Aavani Avittam day alone) who have not yet gone through the formal Brahmopadesam ceremony. On this day, Ramu was given 25 paise coin by Kannamma paatti, while countless freshly prepared *ela vadam*, a soft steamed, rice-based pan cake was served by Suppi aththai who were his paternal grandmother's sister aunt from Needamangalam. Suppi *aththai* (aunt for Ramu's father) was very fond of children. She lived alone near her sister Kannama's house and earned her livelihood by preparing *ela vadam*. Ramu came to know from his relatives that Suppi *aththai's* husband enjoyed all that Kadalankudi Street in Kumbakonam had to offer and neglected her. Tired of husband's wayward ways, Suppi *aththai* had left him. She lived on her own. Although she had every reason to be unhappy and complain about life, she was always happy. Ramu loved to visit her and Kannama *paati*.

During the festival holidays, Ramu learnt to ride his father's bicycle by doing the 'monkey pedal' or the "curing pedal". This helped propel the cycle a distance of about 100 metres or so without assistance. Since his father's bicycle was available for only five minutes before he left for office, Ramu did not progress beyond 100 metres of monkey-pedalling.

A lot happened at Foreshore Estate, from petty theft and quarrels to romance, eloping and even an occasional suicide as well as drowning in the sea. The children in Ramu's family were largely protected from the developments in the neighbourhood, play was discouraged while academic performance was encouraged. But Ramu was a compulsive violator of the rules his mother enforced on him and the other children. He often sneaked out of his house to wander around the area and gather gossip. At times, his mother caught him or his brothers and sisters would rat on him. Whenever he was caught, Ramu diverted his mother's attention by sharing some gossip from the neighbourhood. This helped him get away without punishment. Once he sensed that she was interested in the gossip, he spiced up the original story with quite a few made-up stories. She was so drawn into the story, that she forgave Ramu easily and didn't punish him. The other children, knowing this too well, cautioned their mother. But Ramu's mother was too weak in the face of gossip and powerful story telling.

Time flew. The year was 1971. Ramu joined Santhome Higher Secondary School for class six. Since Ramu was an excellent student, his father requested the headmaster to enroll him in the English medium of education. The headmaster promised Ramu's father to do so the next year, if Ramu stood first in the class six final exam. A year later, Ramu stood first, even among the students of the English medium classes. Ramu's father met with the headmaster and reminded him about his promise. But the headmaster had forgotten his promise. Peeved at this, Ramu's father changed Ramu's school and moved him to St Johns Middle School in Mandaveli. Ramu was quite unhappy about this. After one year at St John's School, Ramu wrote an entrance test for admission into English medium at P. S. High School in the summer of 1973 and joined class eight there. He studied here till the end of class nine.

Ramu had the habit of losing everything – his pens, pencils, geometry box, erasers and tiffin box. Ramu's mother often advised him to be careful with his things but he was always losing them. Her pleas and threats had no effect. She then began punishing him for losing things, but to no avail. Finally she got tired of Ramu's behaviour and told him that he was not going to get lunch anymore. Luckily for him, his teacher, Srinivasan, noticed that he didn't have lunch with him and occasionally bought him *naalana* (25 paise) butter biscuits during lunchtime.

It was early summer of 1975 and Ramu had just completed his ninth standard. His class teacher, nicknamed "apple' by the school boys, was very happy with Ramu as he had won the First Prize in a Thirukkural (couplet) competition at the Tamil Nadu state level competition. He received the prize from the then Chief Minister M. Karunanidhi at the R. R. Sabha Auditorium, Mylapore. Ramu's family was also happy that Ramu had won a state prize. Even his relatives, who usually stayed away, visited Ramu's parents and congratulated Ramu. During one of these visits, Ramu overheard a conversation among his sisters and cousins that their parents were planning to move away from Foreshore Estate to a far-away place called Nanganallur, a developing new suburb of Madras.

His sister's friend, Kalyani, who used to live in Nanganallur, had managed to convince Ramu's parents about the virtues of Nanganallur and what it had to offer to first generation migrants from the rural areas. Ramu's parents were first generation Madras-*vaasis*, with roots in Needamangalam, Kumbakonam and Nagapattinam. They were convinced that they would be more comfortable raising their family in the semi-rural area of Nanganallur. They wanted to bring up their children in the same way they had grown up. They wanted to provide them with fresh milk from the cow and vegetables and fruits grown in their own backyard.

So, one fine day in the summer of 1975, the movers and packers arrived and, soon, Ramu, his brothers and sisters were travelling in an open lorry/truck along with their belongings to Nanganallur. They enjoyed the ride without any protest, all the same wondering what was in store for them in the new place.

Nanganallur... Values Take Shape

Ramu and his family arrived at Nanganallur through the Pazhavanthangal railway gate to a rousing reception. The 'to-be residents' of Nanganallur were entertained by the many trains that passed by the railway level crossing, virtually non-stop. The first lesson was learnt. If you wanted to go anywhere in the city from Nanganallur and return within just a few hours, you must always take the rail-route and not the road-route, as the powerful railway gate stalled anything and everything that passed by, sometimes for hours on end.

Nanganallur is part of the Alandur municipality in Kancheepuram district. It is called Thalakkanaan Cheri in the sub-registrar's land records. Back in 1975, it was a beautiful village with a population of less than 10,000 people. On the south-western and western side of Nanganallur were a few hillocks, which were mined for blue metal that was in huge demand for construction. One of the more popular hillocks is called Thirusoolam, located close to the Chennai Anna International Airport.

Nanganallur, which was then predominantly covered by farm lands, had six main roads and a few houses. Nanganallur was originally a farmland in the early 1970s, with paddy being the principal crop grown round the year.

Big wells provided water for irrigation. Occasionally, the farmers also grew vegetables such as brinjal, ladies finger, bitter gourd, snake gourd and domestic tomato (popularly known as *naatu thakkali*).

In those days, Nanganallur was cut off from the hustle-bustle of the city. It had three railway crossings located about half a kilometre from the Grand Trunk road that connected Chennai to Tiruchi. The first level crossing (the railway crossing was referred to as 'level crossing' in local parlance) was close to the eastern-end of the Meenambakkam airport runway and the Pazhavanthangal railway station, while the other two crossings were near the Meenambakkam railway station and the old Meenambakkam airport (now known as the cargo zone).

Nanganallur was surrounded by beautiful villages, Adambakkam, Puzhithivaakkam and Ullagaram on the north-east and east, Madippaakkam on the south-west, Moovarasanpettai on the south; the Pallavaram and Thrisoolam hillocks on the North-West; Meenambakkam on the north-west and Pazhavanthangal on the north. On the north was the Pazhavanthangal railway station.

On the north-eastern side, there were private houses across twenty streets or so, spread out along the six main roads and around the big *eri* (water tank). This region housed the temples of Rajarajeswari, Hayagrivar, Pillayar and Guruvayurappan. The central part was home to the Accountant General Officers Colony and SIP Colony while the northern part housed the Nehru Colony. Some of the residential areas in the southern, south-eastern and south-western parts were the State Bank Colony, Hindu Colony,

MMTC Colony, AG's Colony, Lakshmi Nagar and Kanniga Colony.

There were quite a few temples in Nanganallur. The discovery of Vishnu sculptures belonging to the Pallava period in 1975, at MMTC Colony, suggests that Nanganallur could have been a place of historical importance. The six feet tall, monolithic granite Vishnu sculpture and other similar sculptures were discovered when the ground was manually dug for building the foundation of a private house. Ramu and his friends were playing cricket when they heard this news from passers-by and they soon swarmed the place to have a look at the beautiful stone sculpture of Vishnu and his cohorts. The sculptures had been buried at least five to six feet into the ground. This brought Nanganallur into the limelight, at least for a few days.

The trains were the main mode of transport in Nanganallur. One could either walk to cycle to a few kilometres to reach the nearest railway stations of Pazhavanthangal (Meenambakkam) and Saint Thomas Mount.

During the rainy season, Nanganallur was largely inaccessible to people living outside, except for those who knew the terrain well. There were a couple of bus routes by which one could enter Nanganallur. A few buses ran on the eastern side of Nanganallur, along the national highway from Velachery to Tambaram, at the Madipakkam intersection. The 18C bus, run by the state transport agency, popularly known as PTC or Pallavan Transport Corporation, negotiated all curves to reach State Bank Colony Extension, on the occasions when the railway gate was open.

Alternatively, one could also exit the national highway at Meenambakkam, cross the Meenambakkam railway station level crossing, take the road along the A. M. Jain college compound, cross the burial ground and enter Nanganallur through one of the streets of Bakthavathsalam Nagar.

This was the more preferred option, as the rainwater drained swiftly along this route. The rainwater flowed from the heart of Nanganallur to the Ullagaram-Puzhuthivaakkam panchayat, through Veerangal *odai* or *vadikaal* (a water drainage canal) to the low lying Pallikkaranai marsh and Thoraipakkam, onto the Bay of Bengal.

Occasionally, an ambassador car or a taxi from the airport could be spotted in Nanganallur. One of the residents, an auditor by profession, owned a big bungalow in the Lakshmi Nagar area. His was the only car in Nanganallur.

Back then Nanganallur was un-motorable during the rainy season. But now things have changed and Nanganallur has seen a lot of development. The locals attributed this to the efforts of one of the chief ministers of Tamil Nadu who in the 'development file' of Nanganallur had written thus: "Anthanar vazhumidam, aavana seiyga", meaning this is "the place where Brahmins live, so do the needful."

Nanganallur had quite a few tanks and lakes such as the Sivan Koil, main market *kulam* (lake) and the Moovarasanpetai *kulam*. The water tanks or the *eris* (the first letter is pronounced like the letter A in the English alphabet) were flooded beyond description during the rainy season. For instance, during the rains, the water from the Thalakkanaan Cheri and Puzhuthivaakkam-Adambakkam lakes flowed across the first main road onto Puzhithivaakkam and Ullagaram and only the brave dared to cross the stream. As school boys, Ramu and his friends often visited these lakes to admire the fury of nature during the monsoons.

The schoolboys were familiar with the entire terrain of Nanganallur. They had come to know every nook and corner of Nanganallur thanks to the pretty girls who lived there and the boys' eternal pursuit of these girls. In fact, the boys found their beauty so alluring that they believed even the angels from heaven, Ramba and Urvasi, paled in comparison. Perhaps this is how Nanganallur got its name – 'nangai' meaning girl and 'nallur' meaning good place, although it would have been more appropriate to have called it Nalnangaiur (the place with good girls). But in those days publicly calling a town the pretty girls' place would have been considered unacceptable and therefore the name Nanganallur instead of Nalnangaiyur. But Ramu felt that the real reason was the men of Nanganallur did not want the outside world to know about Nanganallur's pretty girls. Perhaps they were possessive and did not want to face competition from other men. Maybe this was also the reason why Nanganallur's terrain wasn't so easy to traverse with several lakes, railway crossings and mountains.

There was another reason why the boys knew the terrain well. Many of the households in Nanganallur raised cows and other animals. And during the rainy season, it was the duty of the boys to fetch dried grass straw for the cows. The boys also had to call on veterinary doctors during any emergency such as the birth of a calf. In case the vet was not available, they had to look for the milkman. They also had to bring in bulls for the cows for mating. In the process of running all these errands, the boys got to know the terrain too well.

Ramu had a very interesting and colourful neighbour by name Wentramayar who hailed from Kudavasal. Though he was over 90 years old, he was active and healthy. Ramu's mother insisted that Wentramayar's strength came from doing the Sandhyavandham (a ritual) three times a days and singing *bhajans* (devotional songs) every Saturday evening at the Vara Siddi Vinayaka temple. She also reminded Ramu that his paternal great grandfather Aathivaraha Iyengar also did Sandhyavandanam three times a day. Ramu wondered where Wentramayar found flowing water in water-starved Nanganallur to make the water offering, which was an essential part of the ritual.

Ramu and his younger brothers Mukundhan and Anand were appalled by Wentramayar's mispronunciation of the verses in Vishu Sahasranamam and Thiruppavai, which they knew inside out. But Wentramayar, unmindful of his diction, demonstrated his so-called knowledge of the Dakshina Bhajanai Sampradhayam of Maruthanallur Swamigal and the strength of his vocal cord. He believed he would attain *moksha* (salvation), if the good lord listened to his musical calling.

A typical Saturday *bhajan* session would start with mike testing, followed by *sruthi* (tone) testing. And then the *bhajans* themselves.

Hari Narayana Hari Narayana
Hari Narayana Bhaja Narayana
Bhakta Janapriya Pankaja Lochana
Paramanda Sadasiva Sankara
Paramanda Sadasiva Sankara
Hari Narayana Dharitha Nivarana
Hari Narayana Thavathasoham

....

Sri Dakshinamoorthim BhajarE Manasa

Sri Pakshivaganam BhajarE

....

Mooshika Vagana, Motha ha hastha
Saamara Karnaa Vilambitha Soothra
Vamana Roopa Maheswara Pootra
Vigna Vinayaka Pada NamasthE
Jaya Jaya aaaaahh

....

Jai Janaki Ramana Jai Jai Janaki Ramana
Jai Vibhishana Charana
Jaya Saroruha Sarana Jaya Deena Karunaa
Jaya loka saranya Jaya baktha kaarunya
Jaya Divya lavanya Jaya Jakath Punya
Jai Jaya aaaaahh

....

Mandhara Moole Mathana bhiramam
Bhimbhata ra puri tha venu ganam
Go Go Pa Gopi Janamathya Samastham
Gopam Bhaje Go Kulapurna Chandram
Jai Jai ya aah aah

....

Charanu Charanu Surendra Chanutha

....

Murahara Nakathara Mukundha Madhava
Garuda Kamana Pankaja Naabha Deva
Devesa Gananrathitha Divyam Buja Paatha
Sree Venkata Girinayaka Sree Saa heychariga
Venkatesa Heycharigaa

....

Madhava Bhavathu… Mangalam

....

The *bhajan* session was followed by the *karpura harathi* (a ritual involving lighting the camphor and praying). Although Ramu was wary of Wentramayar's pronunciation, he appreciated his enthusiasm and even offered to play the *kanjira* (a musical instrument) at times. However, in his enthusiasm, Ramu often missed the *tala* (tempo). Wentramayar promptly got rid of him. And Kitcha replaced Ramu.

Kitcha was a perfect accompanist for Wentramayar, but he was afraid of being seen in public as people often asked him about the results of his S.S.L.C exam. Some even had a code name for him, "Mohammed of Gajini".

These *bhajan* sessions never failed to entertain Ramu, as the Seshadris, Sureshs and Rameshs were often seen romancing the Parimalas, Umas and Shyamalas at the fall of night, right outside the Vara Siddhi Vinayaka Swami Temple where the *bhajans* were held. There weren't too many street lights and even the few lamps experienced a voltage drop.

The loud prayers, thanks to Wentramaiyar's vibrant voice, rattled the *mamas* and *mamis glued to the television.* Though it couldn't quite stop the romancing, it did restrain the lovers to certain basic elements and saved their parents from possible embarrassment. Wentramaiyar's voice also dissuaded smooth-operating thieves from getting into their act. Nanganallur was infested with thieves who would unobtrusively walk into homes and walk out with whatever they wanted while *mamas* and *mamis* were hopelessly glued to the television watching either the *Mahabharat* or *Junoon* (a popular Hindi soap dubbed in Tamil).

Ramu had learnt from the *pravachanams* (religious discourses) and the Harikatha that the good lords were often busy with their consorts and a mere prayer would not wake them up from their commitments. Perhaps Wentramayar too knew this and this was the reason for his loud calls to the almighty. Wentramayar's voice was louder than Gajendara, the elephant that screamed its guts out when a crocodile caught his leg at the banks of a river to draw the attention of the lord.

Nanganallur had a few good educational institutions. Konakumbam, in the north-east part of Nanganallur, housed a technical educational institution known as the Konakumbam Institute of Technology. At the Nanganallur-Meenambakkam boundary was the Jain College that served the locals to a good degree. Nanganallur also had a government school, very close to the Pazhavanthangal railway station. Ramu studied class ten and eleven in this school in the Tamil medium. Although his parents wanted him to continue in an English medium school, Ramu rebelled against it for a few reasons.

The nearest English medium school was in Saint Thomas Mount, about 4 km from his house, and Ramu had to commute to school by the 18C bus every day. The headmaster of this school, after interviewing Ramu, suggested that he make a donation of Rs 500 to get admitted in the school. In 1975, one could easily purchase land or a 60 feet by 40 feet plot of ground in Nanganallur with that kind of money. Ramu, who had grown mature and wordly-wise by then, was concerned about his sister Pushpa's marriage. He felt his father could use that money for his sister's wedding, instead of burning all his savings on an English medium education.

Ramu gathered courage and told the headmaster, "*Lanjam Koduppathum, Vaanguvathum Thavaru*" (giving and receiving bribe is an offence), a slogan he had come across in government offices. The headmaster was irritated with the impudence and arrogance of a 15-year-old, that too right in front of his father. He didn't say much and let Ramu's father handle him. And of course, Ramu was denied admission. Ramu's father was furious and told him that he would never accompany him for admission in future.

Ramu was insistent on studying at the government school, which did not offer an English medium of education at that time. Ramu argued that he was fascinated by the method of teaching at the school where students studied under trees, much like in Shantiniketan about which he had read in a book. He had happened to see the students of the government school studying under trees on the day his family moved to Nanganallur.

Soon enough, Ramu and his younger brother were admitted to the Government High School in Nanganallur, in class ten and eight respectively, with the bare minimum admission fee and no donation.

Ramu and his family loved Nanganallur for different reasons. Unlike in the city, here in the suburbs the children got to work in the garden with plants and trees, besides attending to cows. Ramu's father had been raised in a farming community, in Needamangalam, under the careful eyes of his maternal uncle Doraisamy Iyengar, while his mother grew up in Paruthicheery and Nagapattinam under similar surroundings. They taught the children the various ways of rural life and the children picked them up with ease and aplomb.

Although he belonged to the Kaduvankudi village in the Mayavaram taluk, Ramu's father was raised by his uncle. In those days it was common for the mother to bring up her children in her hometown, along with the children's uncle (mother's brother) if the childs father passed away at an early age. Ramu's paternal grandfather, Kaduvankudi Narayana Iyengar, had died following an attack by a wild elephant. He had been on duty as a forest ranger, on the back of a horse, in the Thiruvannamalai range. This meant that Ramu's grandmother, Rukmani Ammal, also known as Sundu, had to return to her brother's place in Needamangalam.

In Needamangalam, Ramu's father learnt the nuances of farming and raising cows while helping his uncle. Ramu's father had his early education in Mannarkudi and did his high school in National High School, Kumbakonam.

Ramu's mother, Renganayaki, grew up with her parents in Nagapattinam. She visited her uncle Parithicheri Dharmasastram Desikachar regularly. Renganayaki's maternal grandfather, Sundaram Iyengar, and her great grandfather, Dharmasastram Krishnamachariar, lived in Paruthicherry, a village near Kumbakonam. In Paruthicherry, she learnt to look after cows and also milk them. It was therefore not surprising that Ramu's parents managed to recreate the Needamangalam-Parithicheri atmosphere in Nanganallur. This meant the entire family got fresh supply of milk, curds, vegetables and fruits for free. Milk was boiled with the help of dried cow-dung (*raati* or *varatti*) that was used as fuel. Ramu's family drank water from the well. They didn't have to depend on the water supplied by the corporation of Chennai.

The children were expected to take care of the cows and their calves. They were treated as part of the family and even given names such as Kalyani, Vellai, Bijili, Padma, Dallan and Nagalakshmi. While Ramu's father worked round the clock and did most of the work, his mother, little brothers, Mukundan and Anand, too chipped in.

Mukundan and Anand could milk the cows, weave coconut leaves and erect a bamboo shed and *pandal* for the gourd plant. They climbed the trees enthusiastically and with ease to pick fruits. Ramu was not inclined to learn all this, but he enjoyed watching his brothers in action.

Ramu was the designated doctor for the cows. He was responsible for forcing bitter medicine down their throat. At times, he helped his father in giving bath to the cows. He also served as the GPS (Global Positioning System) of that time by helping locate the cows when they did not return home on time. Ramu knew the terrain well and he had quite a few friends always ready to help. So if the cows went astray, it was Ramu to the rescue.

Nanganallur was unique in a number of ways. If only one had the time to walk down to the Pazhavanthangal or Meenambakkam railway station, one could enjoy the sight of long-distance trains (especially the Vaigai Express) and electric trains zipping past everything and everyone. Ramu loved watching the powerful trains that his dream job was to become a motorman in one of the electric trains. The nearby Meenambakkam airport was also an interesting place to watch airplanes take off with immense power and noise. Ramu loved Nanganallur and all that it had to offer.

The downside to Nanganallur was there were no good hospitals for human beings or animals, although a handful of doctors did private practice in the 1970s. The roads in Nanganallur were terrible. The joke back then was that any pregnant woman traversing the roads would deliver easily.

Ramu's school, the Nehru Government Higher Secondary School (now known as Jaigopal Garodia Higher Secondary School), was not very demanding. The only challenge was he had to learn all subjects, including Mathematics and Science, in Tamil. Ramu topped the school in the state S.S.L.C. examination, scoring 526 out of 600. He even scored 100 in Algebra and Geometry. But, one of his classmate's mother, bullied the school into displaying her daughter's name as the topper for that year, although she had secured only 516. Ramu, who had by now become a philosopher of some kind, was not flustered by this.

Ramu's mother did not want Ramu to pursue his college education in the city, as she feared city life would corrupt and spoil him. She convinced Ramu to join Jain College in Meenambakkam with Mathematics, Physics and Chemistry as the main subjects.

This was an important point in Ramu's life. Ramu's grandmother, Rukmani Ammal, wished that Ramu study law like her brother N. S. Ramaswamy Iyengar (who was called NS), who practiced law in Mannarkudi and Kumbakonam. She had observed Ramu argue and behave like NS. In fact, she used to call Ramu 'NS.' Ramu's mother disagreed with her; she felt Mathematics was her son's forte and she preferred that he pursue the science stream. Ramu did not have any particular preference though he had a special interest in Mathematics and the challenges it posed.

His only concern was he had to learn everything in English again, as there weren't too many colleges offering education in the Tamil medium. To Ramu's bad luck, within just a month of the college opening for the academic year, its faculty went on strike. They joined several university teachers and abstained from work, demanding better salaries. Their union was called the Madras University Teachers Association (MUTA).

As a result of the prolonged teachers' strike, most of the academic year went by without classes. The students suffered a lot and often referred to MUTA as Madras University Teachers Association Limited or MUTAL, which in Tamil meant foolish people. Ramu managed to learn on his own and passed the university exam in flying colours. He could join any engineering college although there weren't too many engineering colleges to choose from. The colleges were either state run or central government funded; there weren't any private colleges.

The admission to the state government engineering colleges were not only based on the marks obtained in the final exams but was also decided by the candidate's performance in an interview. Ramu attended the interview, with his father anxiously hoping for the best.

The interview was divided into several sections and tested the candidate's knowledge in general affairs, science, and sports. In the sports section, a panel member, who also happened to be a member of the Tamil Nadu legislative assembly, asked him an inappropriate question. "How does your sister look?" This infuriated Ramu no ends and he answered, "Much better than you." As a result, he did not get through the interview and was denied admission into the state government engineering colleges. He had not applied to the central government engineering colleges and his application to arts and science colleges had been turned down as the college authorities felt with the marks he had scored, he would soon give up his seat for a place in an engineering college.

Therefore, he had to wait till admissions to all colleges were completed. A kind professor in Jain College, S. P. Srinivasan, got him admission in the mathematics course in the evening batch. A month later, in consultation with Ramu's mother, Srinivasan moved him to the day batch in the chemistry discipline, much to Ramu's displeasure. However, Ramu excelled in chemistry too, He sailed through college and came in first in his course. The college teachers were very kind and paid personal attention to Ramu and his friends. This left a deep impact in Ramu and he looked at his teachers with great respect and admiration.

During college, Ramu's eldest sister Pushpa's wedding happened. This was an eye-opener for Ramu in many senses as the process taught him many aspects of *lowkikam* or the ways of the real world.

Ramu's father believed in the horoscope. He especially trusted the predictive powers of Karaikudi *josiyar,* (astrologer) a devout Anjaneya/Hanuman *bhakta* in Nanganallur. Ramu's mother, despite being a devout Hindu, was practical about the matters of *lowkikam*, including marriage. But Ramu's father would not accept any marriage proposal till the Karaikudi *josiyar* matched the horoscopes of the girl and the boy and gave his go-ahead.

On one of his visits to the Karaikudi *josiyar's* house, Ramu observed that the *josiyar* scrutinised every statement of his clients under the microscope. Only after a thorough examination of the horoscope, would he pass his judgment. It was no wonder that Ramu's father trusted him. Ramu often accompanies his father to the *josiyar's* house as he enjoyed watching the *josiyar* expose people's false claims.

After three years in under-graduate college, Ramu pursued his master's in a college near his house – the Konakumbam Institute of Technology (KIT), originally called the Sachithanandapuram Institute of Technology at Konakumbam.

Ramu felt ill at ease at KIT as the teachers were not friendly. He missed the personal attention he got at Jain College. Ramu's identity as a poor Tamil Iyengar from the *vadakalai* sub-caste and belonging to the Ahobila mutt was accepted in Jain College. But KIT appeared to be alien territory.

A number of students at KIT were rich and privileged with many of them coming to college in Ambassador cars provided by the government. Many of the students also had music players in their hostel rooms and listened only to loud English music, which was played on late at night. Every Saturday night, the boys marched on to the college open-air theatre to watch a movie in English or Hindi. Not having watched a single movie in his lifetime, Ramu often wondered what the fuss was all about.

Liquor was flowing free in the boys' hostel rooms. Some of them even had physical relationships with their female teachers and hosted girls in their rooms. This was the first of the many culture shocks that Ramu encountered later in life. Ramu felt completely out of place amidst the students and teachers.

Ramu went through the motions at KIT like a lotus leaf in a pond. However, the quality of education at KIT was very good. Later, Ramu often remembered the bicycle ride from Nanganallur to Konakumbam and back, through the coconut groves and the *smashanams* (burial and cremation grounds). Everything else was a blur in his memory.

After two years at KIT, Ramu did a master's in technology at the Satchitanandapuram Institute of Technology in Delhi. In Delhi, everything was strange and new to Ramu, from the language and clothes to the food. He comforted himself by visiting the temples in the morning and evening. This is when he realised the value of his mother's insistence on temple visits. Whenever there was a problem, he went to the temple to seek comfort. He had no difficulty academically and he passed out with high scores in December 1984. Soon after, he joined work as a mud-logging engineer at an oil and natural gas exploring company at Narimanam, very close to Nagapattinam, in the Thanjavur district in Tamil Nadu (now called Thiruvarur district), where he was born. His joy knew no bounds.

Massachusetts... Culture Shock

It was January 1985. Ramu was a happy 23-year-year old working near Nagapattinam, the place where he was born. His company was involved in oil and natural gas exploration in the Cauvery Delta region. His job involved monitoring the quality of dispersion of clay (often called mud) used during drilling for oil exploration.

Ramu got the opportunity to stay in bunkers and work round the clock. While staying in the bunker, Ramu often remembered the stories his grandmother Rukmani Ammal had told him. His grandmother had spent a large part of her life in Needamangalam, Mayavaram (Mayiladuthurai) and Seergazhi. He felt good working in his forefathers' hometown. He hoped his company's exploration in the area brought in jobs for the locals and possibly a lot of oil that would make them rich, as it had with the Arabs.

Ramu found his job too boring, although for the first time in his life he was using instruments about which he had only read in textbooks. He was also given a personal computer from Hewlett-Packard. During his project work for his master's thesis, he had to use a bunch of punched cards and hand it over to the computer centre. Only the next day would he know if his cards were punched free of error and if there was any bug in the programme. And here he was using a computer all on his own. But this did not excite Ramu much. Although the job was not exciting, he had the opportunity to commute to Chennai every fortnight by bus and enjoy a two-week break.

Ramu realised that he was not cut out to be a scientist, as he did not really have the scientific bent of mind and the passion to pursue science. He was not too keen on research. A government job was also ruled out since Ramu's father, who was working as the chief accounts officer in the state government, disliked the idea of Ramu working for the government or the political bosses.

To Ramu, the job at Nagappattinam helped him earn money and that was all he cared about at that moment. Just when Ramu was setting down in his job, his elder brother, Narayanan, began urging him to explore opportunities in the United State of America, where aspiring youth those days went for higher education and better job prospects. Ramu had no intentions of leaving the shores of his country. But Narayanan somehow persuaded Ramu to do his higher studies in the US. In fact, he even generously took care of Ramu's flight expenses and also gave him $500 to meet his initial expenses in the US. Ramu, who had secured admission into a MS degree at the Illinois Institute of Technology, Chicago, bought a one-way ticket to Chicago through New York on TWA airlines.

Ramu boarded the flight from Madras to Bombay (now Mumbai), carrying with him a few months' supply of pickles, *appalam* (*papad*) and *paruppu podi* (lentil powder).

This was not Ramu's first plane journey. He had flown from New Delhi to Madras earlier to attend his second sister Amudha's wedding in November 1984 and therefore he was comfortable on his flight to Bombay. But he was in for a shock on the flight from Bombay to New York, through Cairo.

All the flight attendants were foreigners, their skin so pink like the ones he had seen on the Foreshore Estate beach when he was five or six years old. He could not follow what they were saying although he knew English. What they spoke did not sound like English to him. He didn't understand any of the announcements too. All along the flight, Ramu had severe nausea and he vomited quite a few times. But there was no sign of help from any of the flight attendants.

The airlines had no medicines to offer him and soon the flight attendants were running out of paper bags. This is when Ramu learnt his first American-English word – throwing up (an airline staff had called his vomiting thus). When the flight landed in Cairo for refueling, he got temporary reprieve. Here he requested for some vegetarian food. He was given a plate with what appeared like a crab. The dish had a funny name 'croissant.' Ramu thought that the flight attendant did not understand him.

Struggling to communicate in his 'Tamilised' English to the airline staff, Ramu managed to thank them for the food but politely told them that he could not eat the croissant which appeared like a dressed-up crab. But he had to pay for it. All passengers on board were required to purchase all food items unlike in the Indian airlines where food was free. Ramu already disliked his journey to a new place. He thought to himself – Did the philosophy *athithi devo bhava*? (the guest is equivalent to god) not mean a thing to the TWA management? They were keen on selling anything and everything, except water. More shocks were to follow.

After eighteen hours on the plane, the flight finally landed in New York. All the passengers were required to deplane, collect their luggage, and take an airport shuttle to the domestic airport, if their destination was not New York. Ramu did not understand the announcement clearly as the American accent was too difficult for him to follow.

Ramu was under the impression that all he had to do was to walk from one terminal to another. But he was totally off the mark. The New York airport was unbelievably vast. He had seen nothing like that in his life. Planes were taking off and landing at such great frequency, the kind of which he had not seen even at the crowded railway stations in Madras. There were so many planes on the ground, many more than the number of vans parked during big political rallies in Madras.

Ramu had to pick up his baggage for onward journey from the conveyor belts on the ground floor. It took him quite a while to even locate the conveyor belt to collect his two boxes. The hand-pushed trolley was available free in Indian airports, while in the New York airport one had to pay to use them. He observed passengers pushing a dollar note into a vending machine to unlock the hand trolley. But he didn't have a dollar on him and he was too afraid to ask anyone for any help. So he dragged the boxes to the immigration counter with all the might his weak muscles could summon.

There were many immigration counters marked 'for US citizens only' and 'for passengers with a foreign passport.' Ramu located his counter. The immigration official quizzed him on a number of issues. But all Ramu could manage as a reply was a blank stare as he could not follow any of the questions. Finally, after getting his visa papers, passport and immigration card stamped, he was directed to the customs counter.

There he was instructed to open all his boxes. After a thorough examination of the boxes, the customs officials pulled out the plastic bags containing dry eatables and wet pickles. They allowed him to carry the dry items and trashed the pickles. Ramu was so heart-broken to lose the *aavakkai* (mango) pickle painstakingly prepared by his mother. She had made them with great care, attention and love. It was almost as if he was losing his mother. But there was no room for sentiments and the tough customs officials were very strict with Ramu and demanded he leave the place.

Soon, Ramu was out in the open. He decided to walk to the domestic terminal in his own imitable Indian style, dragging all his possessions from one terminal to another, blissfully unaware of the distance he had to walk and the time it could take. He was diffident about talking to people given his understanding of American English. Nobody seemed to pay any attention to him. Ramu followed his instincts and occasionally referred to the display boards. Fortunately, the airport was organised and he had little trouble in finding his way.

As he walked from the international terminal to the domestic terminal, along the corridors of the J.F.K Airport, he kept hearing a siren from some location, which he assumed was coming from outside the airport. It was continuous and there seemed to be no end to it. The only siren that Ramu had heard in India was during the India-Pakistan war. Ramu felt this was ironic, as the airport seemed like a battlefield. The siren really scared him. He

held on to his baggage tightly. Ramu finally managed to reach the domestic terminal from which a local TWA flight would take him to Chicago.

Ramu reached the counter and showed his ticket. The service person informed him that the flight was delayed due to a technical snag and it was scheduled to leave about eight hours later. Now, Ramu had not eaten for nearly 20 hours and was terribly hungry. Whatever he saw at the food stalls, though nicely displayed, appeared like crabs or frogs or some creepy-crawly creature, with an occasional blood-red topping.

Finally, he decided to call his classmate, Sri, who had been living in Chicago for a few years. Sri had explained to Ramu, in a letter (in the pre e-mail days, this was the most inexpensive and sure way of communicating with anyone in the US), that Ramu should carry with him several 'quarters' to make phone calls from the public telephone booths at the airport lounge.

Ramu dropped a quarter and followed the written instructions displayed on the public telephone and dialled Sri's number. He could hear Sri say "hello" at the other end and before he could hear anything more, Ramu thought he heard some 'cross talk.'

In the 1980s, the Indian telephone system, which Ramu was used to, had a 'free service.' It was common to hear conversations between other people and this made for interesting gossip. It was commonly called 'cross talk.' So when he heard 'cross talk' in the US airport, Ramu felt at home though he could not follow the conversation. But then, he could not hear anything from Sri and then the telephone connection got cut.

Ramu used another quarter to call Sri again. After establishing contact and exchanging a few more sentences, Ramu heard the 'cross talk' again. Ramu ignored it only to end up in another disconnected call. This happened a few times and he was running out of quarters. Finally, Ramu looked around to see if anyone could help. There were quite a few people around and he thought of approaching an elderly man for help.

The old man was engaged in an intimate moment with a woman young enough to be his daughter. But Ramu didn't think it was inappropriate to interrupt him. He approached the old man with a polite, "Excuse me sir. Can you please help me?" The old man ignored him. Ramu persisted and the old man became furious and began to yell. A startled Ramu wondered why his polite enquiry had annoyed the old man. Only years later did he realise that in the West, it was rude to disturb people who were expressing themselves passionately in public. It violated their private space and fundamental freedom.

Finally, Ramu managed to get four quarters in exchange for a dollar note and he called Sri. This time, Sri told him, at the first instant, that what he had heard earlier was a recorded message telling him he had run out of talk-time and must add another quarter to continue.

Only after a few months of living in the US did Ramu realise that what he thought was 'cross talk' was actually from the telephone company that was monitoring the duration of the call. In India one could talk endlessly in a public telephone booth for just eight *anas*, while scores of people would wait restlessly outside the booth. But in the US, telephone systems worked differently.

His early experiences in the US made Ramu realise that bookish knowledge and scoring high marks in an English medium college meant little. His college hadn't prepared him for the reality around him, which was tougher than he imagined it to be. He realized that he may have basic knowledge of the English language but American English and customs were much too confusing, He had managed to pass the spoken and written TOEFL test (Test of English as a Foreign Language) conducted by the English Language Testing Society, US but had trouble getting by with his English in the US. Ramu was not adequately prepared to meet the challenges and assumed that things worked the same way as they did in India.

The TWA flight to Chicago started around 9 p.m. and reached O'Hare International Airport at around 11 p.m. After landing, Ramu waited along with others to receive his on-board luggage. He struck a conversation with a middle-aged person, also from Tamil Nadu. After collecting his bags, Ramu explained his situation and requested him to help him get a private taxi, as it may be too late to take the public transport. The middle-aged man expressed his inability to help and told him that it was easier to just follow the instructions on display.

Ramu had not been brought up by his parents to be independent. He was petrified about finding his way around the O'Hare airport, which appeared as big as the J.F.K. Airport in New York. He was physically and mentally tired and wanted someone to help him find the 'taxi stand.' As stepped outside the airport, he was lost. It was around midnight. Suddenly Ramu heard somebody talk to him, in another kind of American English accent. Ramu could not understand what he said and was frightened by his appearance.

The stranger was an African-American, about six feet and six inches tall. Initially, Ramu refused his offer; he could not understand why this 'stranger' was offering to help him. The 'stranger' followed him. Soon, they passed by an old woman and the 'stranger' spoke to her. From their conversation, Ramu managed to understand that the 'stranger' was a cab (taxi) driver.

The stranger turned towards Ramu and asked him if he would get into his cab for one hundred dollars. Ramu had no choice but to accept the offer. At that moment, the money did not sound big to him. In India, night-time taxi fares cost a few hundred rupees. Besides, he was really tired and hungry and wanted to get to some place to eat and rest.

Ramu agreed to the fare and in no time the cab driver lifted Ramu's luggage, two suitcases and a handbag, and started to walk as though he was just carrying shopping bags. Ramu walked behind him and so did the old lady. Soon, Ramu saw a huge parking lot with hundreds of cars. It was an underground parking lot. The driver drove very fast by Indian standards. Although there were many traffic signals, the driver obeyed each one of them, unlike in India were drivers assumed that traffic signals were meant to be broken.

Soon, the taxi got into what appeared to be the highway to heaven. Ramu had not seen anything like this. The road was well-lit with neat lanes. Cars and huge trucks were zipping through as though it was a busy production facility. Ramu was astonished, shocked and excited all at once. The car zoomed through at a very high speed. The meter, unlike in India, increased dollar by dollar. After about 30 minutes, the driver got out of the highway, slowed down and entered the city with a number of streets.

Finally, the cab reached the woman's destination. For Ramu, it was another ten minutes of driving through the highway and local roads before the driver pulled over in front of the address that Ramu had shown earlier. It was 2 a.m. The apartment complex in which his friend lived was not open and Ramu did not know what he had to do to enter inside. Thankfully, the cab driver helped him. He looked at the door number and pressed a button. After nearly five minutes, someone said something over the microphone and Ramu answered. Finally, the main door opened (it was locked electronically and only the resident of the apartment could open it) and Ramu got in. Ramu took out a hundred dollar note from his wallet, handed it over to the driver, and thanked him profusely.

The driver asked him something that sounded like, "Are you not going to tip me, man?" Ramu had not heard of the word 'tip' but the body language of the driver indicated that he wanted more money. This was typical of taxi and auto drivers in Chennai. Ramu gave him ten extra dollars. The driver walked away, without yelling or cursing like they did in Chennai. Ramu searched through the apartment numbers and reached the second floor to Sri's apartment. Sri asked Ramu why it took him so much time to get there.

Ramu did not want to narrate his ordeal. It would only show how incapable he was in following instructions. Over curd rice with pickle, Ramu had a brief chat with Sri and then went to bed, thinking of his parents, brothers, sisters and even the cows, calves, and the other people of

Nanganallur that he had left behind. He woke up the next day, his first Sunday in the US, with a resolve to help new student visitors to the universities in the US, once he had settled in.

Ramu was to join the Illinois Institute of Technology (IIT) on Monday. He took the local bus on 7200 Michigan Avenue, along with his friend Sri, and reached IIT on 3100 Michigan Avenue. After completing a few formalities, Ramu was allotted a room in the hostel, called fraternity in local parlance. The fraternity had two sections, one for the men and another one for the women. The area where the rooms were located was under electronic surveillance and one had to swipe a card to enter. It would lock automatically after one entered in. After checking into his room, Ramu decided to have a bath. As he entered the corridor leading to the bathrooms, he was in for another shock.

The boys were walking around naked in the corridor, as well as in the bathroom. Ramu went back to his room and began crying, wondering if his decision to come to the US was right. After some time, Ramu made up his mind that no matter what his surroundings were, he would continue to do what was comfortable to him. Frankly, there was nothing he could do to change his surroundings.

Soon, it was lunchtime. Ramu went to the dining hall only to find a wide variety of unskinned animal parts in all forms and shapes. Even the so-called vegetarian food items were coloured and shaped unusually or with toppings that looked suspect. The only thing that Ramu could consume without any risk was apple and orange juice. But the orange juice was very bitter. Later, Ramu learnt that there was a difference between orange juice and orange drink.

Just over a day in the US and already Ramu felt sick, frustrated and clueless. He decided to go for a walk around the fraternity. On the way, he came across a small shop called '7-eleven' which claimed to be open '24 hours.'

The shop was nearly ten times the size of his two-bedroom house in Nanganallur. Ramu bought a carton of chocolate milk and hot potato fries. He sat in a corner to consume it. Ramu had found a way to address his appetite in a safe and acceptable manner. Chocolate milk and potato chips became his staple diet for the next 30 days. Ramu felt at home in 7-eleven.

Classes started the next day and Ramu got in touch with quite a few enterprising Indian students who had done their home-work before coming to Chicago. They were also exposed to the American culture and way of life through cinema. Ramu had not seen any movies in his life in any language.

Soon, with the help of his new Indian acquaintances, Ramu left the 'notorious' fraternity house to share an apartment with three others. Slowly, Ramu began to feel confident about his stay in the US.

The apartment had three bedrooms in different sizes. One bedroom was very large with an attached bathroom. The other two bedrooms were smaller and had a shared bathroom. Ramu and his two housemates agreed to pick the room by drawing lots. G got the biggest room; Ramu got the medium-sized one, while the smallest room went to P. Though they had unanimously agreed to draw lots, P was unhappy. He complained that he had got a raw deal.

The enterprising G, who was more broad-minded compared to the others, brought to the house a new acquaintance, S from Bangladesh, who was more experienced. S was warm, friendly and took great pleasure in helping the Indians. He drove Ramu around to shopping malls where Ramu bought non-stick pans, a few kitchen appliances and grocery. Ramu's mother had packed a whole lot of items including a pressure cooker and a cookbook for beginners *Samaithu Paar* (learn to cook) by Lifco Publications. Ramu had no difficulty starting his small experiments in cooking. Ramu's housemates did not dare to experiment and just assisted Ramu in minor chores. They ate whatever Ramu cooked. Ramu cooked mostly fried rice with peas during the week. During the weekends, he tried out more elaborate recipes. P visited his relatives in suburban Chicago during the weekend for food and rest.

The three housemates drew up a few rules for maintaining the house, as services of maids were too expensive and not common in the US. They agreed to take turns to clean the house, kitchen and the bathrooms. While Ramu followed the rules sincerely, he soon realised that no one else was. Each one kept blaming the other and as a result the bathrooms became dirty over time. The kitchen was full of grime and stains from using oil and Indian spices.

The apartment manager, on the first day that they moved in, had told them that often Indians did not maintain the houses well and cautioned them to take care of the apartment properly. The manager had been right. Ramu was frustrated and irritated with his housemates.

The concepts of 'dignified' and 'less dignified' labour were deeply rooted in his house mates. Though Ramu had not done any of these chores in India, such as cleaning the toilets and kitchen, sweeping and vacuuming the floors, and doing the laundry, he had no difficulty adapting to the new lifestyle.

Ramu's apartment mates seemed to have deep personal prejudices and did not really care about the house, as long as the menial labour was done by someone else. Ramu ended up doing all the work, all the time.

Meanwhile, G made new friends and had a busy social life. He was the first one of the three housemates to take up driving lessons. Ramu was not quite outgoing and preferred staying at home studying, cooking and listening to music. They had taken up another housemate, N, who introduced Ramu to the *ghazals* of Mehdi Hassan and Ghulam Ali and the Gurbani (from the Holy Granth of the Sikhs).

At times, Ramu visited the temples in Arora and Lemonte, as he did not like to watch television to kill time. Television shows just showed what Ramu saw on the streets of Chicago every day – ambulances and speeding police vehicles with their siren. Plus news channels were full of news of murders and showed gory visuals from the murder scene. This disturbed him a lot. In India, people watched television to escape from reality. Moreover, there were fewer violent crimes and murders in India.

Ramu did not feel safe to walk on the streets of Chicago, where people were often mugged (robbed at knife/gun point). Ramu had been mugged by two African-American kids right in front of the African-American and European-American police. Especially unsafe was the downtown area. Public transportation (bus or the elevated train) was also not safe any time of the day. Mugging happened in full view of people and everyone was a mute spectator.

In India, Ramu was used to people begging but mugging was a whole new scary phenomenon. Some of the beggars in India were convinced that begging was a legitimate method of earning a livelihood. While some beggars were persuasive, a few conned you too. But it was not violent and forceful like the kind Ramu experienced in Chicago. Ramu's friends had warned him that he must always be ready to part with a dollar or two but what Ramu was not sure how many times he had to part with money before reaching his destination safely. There were muggers at every point.

On two occasions, the 'muggers' did not even demand money, but they pointed a sharp object at the back of his neck and simply walked away with his purse. They pocketed the money and discarded the purse a few yards away along with his identity card. This was a problem unique to the city, and the suburbs were relatively safe. But Ramu could not afford a room in the suburban area. Besides, Ramu's workplace was in the city. So a small part of his monthly budget was reserved for muggers.

Ramu's studies were progressing well; he had passed all the tests with outstanding grades. He had managed to get his social security card from the Federal Government office in Chicago and this experience was not very different from what he had encountered in some of the government offices in Inda. The faculty at his institute was happy with Ramu. But Ramu was feeling insecure and unsafe in Chicago. His Indian friend J (who introduced him to lovely Malayalam songs) had once told him that the university in the suburbs was safe. Therefore, Ramu decided to move to a university located in the suburbs the next academic year.

About six months passed in Chicago and Ramu had earned enough to buy a second-hand Mazda for one thousand dollars. With the mandatory insurance and receipt, Ramu registered the car in his name. A Taiwanese classmate of Ramu drove the car from the owner's house to the parking lot in Ramu's apartment complex. Ramu wrote a small poem following the *ethugai* and *monai* grammar structure (poetry that rhymes) to his friend Sarathi in Nanganallur, enclosing a picture of the Mazda.

"Pinnakkam emmakkum Pallavan thanakkum

Pirakkum pinnar pazhiya car mayakkam."

This roughly translates as (although it is difficult to make the translation rhyme): "Earlier my attachment was with the Pallavan Transport Corporation bus, but now I have fallen far old cars."

Even as Ramu adapted himself to the new lifestyle, he was also getting tired of the rigid rules. Back home there were hardly any rules and everything was some form of an 'adjustment.' Here in the US, every source of income and purchase was taxed in some form or the other. Ramu foolishly decided to rebel against the rules and do what he pleased. He would face the consequences later, if caught.

Ramu decided to learn driving on his own. The consequences of getting caught, the hefty fine he would have to pay, and the risk of damaging other vehicles on the road did not deter him one bit. Back in India, driving licences could be easily bought, without even demonstrating the knowledge of road rules or the ability to handle a motor vehicle. The motor vehicle act existed only on paper in his country. Ramu remembered a film song featuring actor M. G. Ramachandran.

"Clutch-i mithithu, Gear-i thalli, accelerator-i azhuthanum;

Steering-i pudichu, horn-i azhuthi, pa paam endru shokka ottanum;

Samyathil brake-i-um pidikkanum."

Hold the clutch, apply the gear and press the accelerator. Hold the steering and sound the horn. Drive in style and apply the brakes when the need arises. This is how the drivers of the state-run buses in Madras drove the vehicles. And he decided to do the same.

At night, Ramu began to drive the car, the MGR song guiding him through the way. He drove without using the horn. Americans rarely used the horn. It was considered rude road behavior and unless one wanted to be caught, the horn was seldom used.

Initially, Ramu found it scary to drive on his own. Soon, he learnt to manoeuvre the car without stalling it. After a few weeks of intense practice, Ramu was good to go. He went to the Registry of Motor Vehicles (equivalent to the Regional Transport Office in India) and wrote a test. He was issued a learning permit. Ramu began driving the car on the roads around his apartment complex, making right turns wherever necessary (In the US, the convention is to drive on the right side of the road). After several days of practice, Ramu felt confident to take up the driving test.

A friend of Ramu drove his car to the motor vehicles office at the appointed time (everything in the US happened according to prior appointments, including hair-cuts, doctor visits, and even burying the dead.). The official conducting the driving test was a tall and hefty man, who dwarfed Ramu. He pronounced Ramu's name as Ram-U.

It sounded as though he was asking Ramu if he was going to ram the car. He sat next to Ramu in his car, shuffling in discomfort as there was no leg-room for a tall man like him. He instructed him to do a few manoeuvres, including a three-point-turn.

The road test inspector (that is how he was called) had a hand gun strapped to his belt. Ramu felt nervous. In India, the police didn't wield anything except a *lathi* and they didn't appear so scary.

As luck would have it, Ramu did not understand the test inspector's instructions. Just five minute into the road test, the road test inspector told Ramu that he had to reappear for the test, after better preparations. It took Ramu a few more months to get the next appointment. And this time, he passed the test thankfully. Later Ramu learnt that except for the best of drivers, no one was given a licence at the first instance.

Armed with the licence, Ramu drove his car on the highway. He experienced an adrenaline rush as he zipped down the ramp joining other cars and trucks on the road, cruising at a speed of 55 miles per hour. Initially, Ramu was intimidated by the trucks. Eventually, he got used to them.

Many of his classmates still had not learnt driving. So Ramu felt thrilled at his new-found freedom. Now he need not fear muggers. The car gave him a new lease of life, as Ramu was free to move around Chicago fearlessly.

During his one-year stint in Chicago, Ramu witnessed and experienced several things that were not acceptable to him. On one occasion, he saw an African-American making out in the open, behind his university compound. He was shocked out of his wits. On another occasion, Ramu saw two white students expressing their desire for each other, in front of the University of Chicago library, well past midnight.

On Saturday mornings, it was common to see broken beer bottles on the street side, especially around 31 and State Avenue. Ramu found the way women in the US dress very 'provocatively.' Their clothes, Ramu felt, revealed more than what they concealed. Unlike in India, where women's clothing was dictated by what society considered 'appropriate' and 'acceptable,' with a huge emphasis on guarding one's 'modesty.'

At times, when he felt emotionally out of place, Ramu went to the Indian town known as Devon Street. Here, Ramu was at home, especially at an Indian restaurant where he ate to his heart's content. During one such visit to the restaurant he was happy to observe that the food inspector was taken care of by the Indian owner of the restaurant in the typical Indian way and this experience was enough to realize that officials were amenable and friendly to business in places outside India too.

As a past time, Ramu took up bowling. That was the only new sport that Ramu could pick up in Chicago. But since that was quite expensive for a student on a fellowship, he couldn't go bowling too often.

Soon, Ramu received a fellowship to pursue Ph.D at the University of Massachusetts at Amherst. Ramu was relieved to be leaving Chicago and its high voltage life for a safer and sedate life in the countryside. He packed all his things in his Mazda and set about for the long drive to Amherst. Ramu drove for 19 continuous hours, taking a break only for food and coffee. He reached Buffalo at around three in the morning. Suddenly, he heard a loud honk from a nearby truck. Ramu woke up with a jolt. He had briefly fallen asleep due to the monotony of driving alone. He was also tired from the long drive. His Mazda was on the service lane (or shoulder) and was not accelerating. Ramu thanked the truck driver for waking him up. He took some rest, drank a cup of coffee and after another eight hours drive, he reached Amherst at noon.

Amherst was a beautiful and quiet town. Ramu felt safe from the very beginning. There would be no mugging or loud sirens from ambulance or police vehicles here.

Life in Chicago had prepared him to adapt to any new place. Ramu finished all the requirements for an M.S. degree in one semester much to the surprise of his faculty advisor who found Ramu academically brilliant. The Ph.D. programme had several events that made socializing easy. Every Friday evening, there was a seminar followed by the happy hour where faculty and students met over soft drinks, donuts and potato chips. Soon, the senior students warmed up to the juniors and took them out to the nearby bar for beer. Once a week, in the summer months of July to September, the entire department played 'Ultimate Frisbee.' The American students in the lab were friendly and interacted with Ramu a lot. Many of them were curious to know from Ramu why in India many people suffered from hunger despite having so many cows.

When Ramu heard this for the first time, he did not quite understand what they were saying. Only later did he understand that they were referring to the cow as food. His American friends, who had seen shows on India on television, did not understand why hunger was an issue when 'food' was roaming freely on the streets. To Ramu, a Hindu, the cow was a sacred animal and had to be protected. But to the American, the cow was food.

At graduate school in Amherst, most American students had a boyfriend or girlfriend. They had physical intercourse without any qualms whereas in India, sex before marriage was considered a taboo. In India, sex was an act to be engaged in post marriage in the privacy of one's bedroom.

The casual manner in which young men and women gave in to their physical needs made Ramu question his values. Though he was initially shocked, Ramu slowly began to understand that different cultures thought and behaved differently and there was no need to consider one superior to the other. He looked at everything with an open mind but did not have the courage to explore or experiment.

The world around him was open and liberal. This helped him overcome his inhibitions and appreciate all kinds of cultures and beliefs. He began to enjoy Hindustani music, ghazals, north Indian food and practices. He started watching Tamil movies and even liked a few of them. Slowly, he started appreciating American folk music, country music and the music of Bob Dylan, Woodie Guthrie, Arlo Guthrie, Pete Seeger and Beatles. He also took an interest in baseball, American football and basketball.

Ramu began to watch a lot of American television shows, especially cartoons. He also read up on American history and politics. Pizza, donut, French fries, potato wafers, burrito, chimichanga, quesadilla, coke and subs were no longer unfamiliar to his taste buds. Apart from visits to temples and museums, Ramu also travelled extensively around America… Cricket, workouts at the gym and research ensured that his average day was packed to the hilt.

After three years in the US, Ramu for the first time began enjoying the American experience. Just when Ramu was getting lost in the American way of life, an odd incident or two would remind him of his Indian identity.

Ramu lived with Ani (an Indian) and Jack, (a first generation Irish American), in Northwood Apartments in Sunderland. Ramu enjoyed cooking. Ani and Ramu took turns cooking dinner. Ramu often made *sambar* and potato fry, as potato was one of the most abundant vegetables in the US. Dinner was usually ready by six in the evening, after which he went out for a walk till Ani returned from the university. They would then have dinner together.

As the days progressed, Ramu realised that the quantity of potato was not enough for them. One day, Ramu asked Ani if he had eaten some potato curry before dinner and Ani replied in the negative. Ani was a very smart person and he asked, "Hey Ramu, did you check with Jack?" To which Ramu said, "These American guys cannot handle our spices." Ani then replied, "You will be surprised."

As the discussion went on, Jack stepped out of his room. On his way out, Ani asked him, "Jack, did you taste the potato curry?" Jack responded, "Yeah. I thought you guys were done with dinner." After Jack left, Ani and Ramu decided to make more potato curry (two kilos per day) for dinner so that Jack could have his share too. This led to Jack bringing all his Irish girl friends for dinner. Soon enough the two kilos rose to four or five kilos of potato curry on Friday nights, all of which vanished in no time.

One day, in the middle of the night, a cop woke up Ramu and his house-mates and told them they had to search the house. Ramu and Ani agreed, although Jack protested and asked for a search warrant.

Ramu and Ani requested Jack to keep quiet as both of them were scared of the gun-trotting policeman. Ramu had a terrible cough and fever and was not very pleased with the late night raid. A minute later, their neighbour Martha, a young woman, appeared in their apartment and profusely apologised to them for the inconvenience. She informed Ramu, Ani and Jack that Susy had disappeared and that she had called the cops to find her. Ramu and Ani were perplexed and assumed that Susy must be a dog or cat. Jack was thoroughly disturbed.

Martha went into Ramu's room and a minute or two later she came out screaming with joy. "We found her, we found her! How can you do this to me, Susy? Come on sweetie!" The cop was relieved that the search had ended finally.

The young lady began kissing Susy who lay coiled, nice and tight. Ramu and Ani were shell-shocked to see that Susy was a python, about five feet long. She had been found under Ramu's bed.as Ramu kept his thermostat at a cozy 80 F. Americans rarely turned the heater in their room and the snake being a tropical dweller like Ramu selected his room and the area below his bed to rest. After that incident, Ramu slept on top of the dining table in the living room

A few years later, Ramu came to know that a python, raised as a pet by a research scholar in the department of physics and astronomy, had accidentally killed him by strangling him. Ramu shuddered and was glad that Susy had not strangled him in his sleep.

At Amherst, Ramu started a cricket team with several Indians and a few students from England, Australia and the West Indies. The university permitted the students to use its playground on North Pleasant street during the summer months, as long as they maintained decorum.

Every Friday, the team practiced cricket with Kookaburra balls from Australia and proper cricketing gear. The games ended at eight at night, as there was still plenty of light. One Friday, after a practice game, Ramu was driving down the North Pleasant street towards his house when he was stopped by a cop. Ramu pulled over to the curb and stopped the car, with his hands still over the steering wheel for the cop to see. The cop asked him for his driver's license and insurance papers. Ramu opened the dash-board, after seeking the cop's approval to open the same and showed all the documents to the cop.

The cop asked him a few more questions and Ramu showed him his student identity issued by the university. The cop did not appear to be convinced. Just then two more police patrol vehicles arrived, flashing light on either side of his car. The cops who had just arrived searched the rear of his car and suddenly Ramu heard one of them saying, "That is a cricket ball!"

Once they were convinced, they let him drive away. Before leaving, Ramu asked the cops why he was held up. One of the cops, who happened to be an Irishman, explained to Ramu that the American cop had mistaken the cricket ball for a hand grenade and had called his back-up team for help. Ramu couldn't help smiling and thanked god for sending an Irish cop to the scene. He had saved him from a possible embarrassment.

Ramu's youngest brother, Anand, joined him in 1988 and life in the US got better. One day, Ramu and Anand were chatting with a bunch of friends over dinner. In the course of their conversation, Anand and Ramu told their friends that in the US, Indians had no knowledge of religious verses and that they could recite the lyrics of Tamil film songs in temples and no one would even notice. Their friends retorted that Tamil speaking people in the US knew the difference and would certainly not fall for the trick.

Ramu and Anand took it up as a challenge to prove they were right. Soon, Ramu, Anand and his friends went to Maryland on a short vacation. At Maryland, they visited a temple. When everyone was gathered around the *sannidhi*, Ramu and Anand rendered a Tamil film song in the same tune in which the Nallayira Divya Prabhandam (a collection of 4,000 verses in Tamil) is rendered.

Ramu: Aatha aathorama vaaraiya, paatha paarkamale poraiya

Anand: Akkam pakkam yaarum illai alikkalam vapillai

Nala nenjai naam thozhuthom namuda namperumaan"

Alimaathar olganina aayiram tholudaya.

Nobody noticed anything odd. Ramu's friends were impressed but they wanted Ramu and Anand to prove it again. The next day there were more people at the temple.

This time, Ramu and Anand sang another Tamil film song.

Ramu: Anthamaanai parungal azhagu, ilampaavai enodu vuravu

Anand: Anthapennai thalaatum illamai intha paavai kan thoovum pannier.

The audience thought the words were in praise of the lord and not from a movie song. After that incident, Ramu and Anand's friends never dared to challenge them on matters of Indians' culture.

During the spring of 1989, Ramu had to go to Florida to make a research presentation. He had prepared all the material on transparent sheets (slides were just making their entry and a PowerPoint presentation was unheard of). Ramu boarded the flight at Hartford, Connecticut. It was not a direct flight to Miami; the plane had a stop-over in Cincinnati, Ohio. Since there was plenty of time during the journey, Ramu opened his bag and took out the transparencies to go over the presentation material.

At the airport, Ramu ran into an old friend of his. Since his flight to Miami would not take off for some more time, they both had a cup of coffee in the lounge. His friend asked him about his big Colombian moustache. Ramu told him he began sporting a big moustache to feel more manly and powerful.

Ramu spent a week in Miami with an old friend, Rajasekar Bala, who had studied with him in KIT. Miami was a tourist centre. There was so much to do there and tourists invariably returned home with an empty wallet. Ramu had a great time visiting Orlando, Sea World, the museum and the crocodile park. He then flew back to Hartford.

When he got out of the plane at Hartford, a group of men flashing metal badges asked Ramu to step aside. Ramu could not read what was written on the badge but he guessed they were some kind of law enforcement people.

He had grown confident and assertive in three years and he demanded to know whom they were. The officers refused to reply and moved him to a secluded room in the airport premises.

Since these areas were not meant for passengers, Ramu sensed he was in trouble. Once inside the room, he was asked to display his identity. His bag was thoroughly searched but the officers could find nothing incriminating. Ramu requested permission to make a phone call to his Ph.D. supervisor. But his request was turned down. He was interrogated for about twenty minutes and at the end of it the officers let him leave the airport.

Ramu wondered why he had been targeted. He politely asked the officers why he was detained. The officers told him that his movements had been monitored since he looked like a Colombian. Moreover, he was travelling to Miami, which was infamous for drug peddlers. The flight stewards had informed them that Ramu was inspecting some material carefully, opening and closing his baggage frequently during the journey to Miami. He was also seen exchanging something with someone at Cincinnati airport.

This incident at the Hartford airport and another similar incident at the Boston Logan airport shook him. He realised that when in America he should present himself like an American – clean-shaven and wearing a three-piece suit with a tie.

While in Amherst, Ramu and his friends visited all the Indian temples and attended many music concerts during the weekends. Ramu also made friends with a few elderly Indians, whom the Americans called 'senior citizens.' They were primarily visiting their daughters to help them take care of their babies. Though they were happy to be with their grand-children, they also felt depressed and bored in the suffocating American apartments and social settings. They missed good old India. Nevertheless, they felt it was their 'duty' to help their daughters in need.

Ironically, though they felt ill at ease in America, on returning to India the 'senior citizens' could not stop gushing about the great American life and how India was still lagging behind in everything. Obviously, they didn't want to admit that they felt 'used' by their children.

During his interactions with Indians in the US, Ramu realised that though most of them said they wanted to return to India, they had no intentions of doing so. Most of them, so used to the pleasures and comforts of the US, wanted During the interactions with the men and women settled in the USA, Ramu and Anand learned the real meaning of "thriunaalai povar charithram" (will go tomorrow). Most of the men would confess that they had intentions of returning to India and even threatened so by sending an application or so for job. The fact was that a vast majority of them wanted to settle down in that country.

Many years later, Ramu was driving back home along with his friend and his wife, after visiting another friend Kumar at the University of Illinois at Urbana-Champagne. They had driven about 100 miles when Ramu noticed that his car was low on gas (petrol in Indian parlance). Soon, they found a signboard stating that the nearest gas station was ten miles from the next exit. Ramu drove down the next exit and followed the directions to the gas station. Even after driving for miles, he could not find the gas station.

Ramu became desperate, as there wasn't enough fuel. In a typical Indian way, they stopped their car in front of a house, walked through the gate and knocked on the front door.

There was no response although the lights and the television were on. After some time, they heard a woman's voice, "Hold your hands up and do not move." Ramu and his friends, taken by surprise, obeyed her implicitly. The woman, who held a shot gun in her hand, ordered them to turn around and walk out of the house, into their car. They did so without protesting. Somehow, Ramu gathered courage and told the woman, "We have nearly run out of gas. All we want to know is where the nearest gas station is."

The woman, with her gun still pointing at Ramu and his friends, told them to drive about two miles to the right. After driving for a few minutes, they found a gas station. They filled up the tank with gas and drove out of the neighbourhood onto the interstate highway. Ramu learnt another lesson. Trespassing on someone else's property, even for a genuine reason, was simply a no-no in the US.

It was the year 1987. Ramu, who had been living in the US for over two years, began to miss home. It was time to visit India, for which he had been saving for the last two years.

Ramu visited Madras in the month of December. He could not believe that the Madras airport had changed so dramatically. The airport was noisy and bustling with busy people who seemed to have little regard for others, much like in the American airports.

Surely, this was not the place he had grown up in, he thought to himself. As he left the airport in a taxi, Ramu noticed a poster that said ‘Kaalani Ilavasa Thittam.’ Ramu asked his father whether the Government was giving away ‘colony’ (colloquial term for a residential area) free to people and if so where did the funds come from. Ramu’s father was quick to point out *kaalani* meant footwear. He also remarked that perhaps Ramu had forgotten his Tamil.

Ramu’s friends and relatives noticed several changes in Ramu’s behavior and teased him. For instance, Ramu was always polite to people and said ‘thank you’ to the auto-rickshaw driver, the bus driver and the flower and milk vendors. They thought that something had come over Ramu and told him it was crazy to thank people for their services.

During his visits to Madras once in two years, Ramu fell sick with cold and cough. His immunity dipped and he developed frequent allergies, which lasted the entire month’s stay. Despite having a tough time adjusting to the Indian conditions, Ramu enjoyed his vacation, revisiting his favourite spots and getting pampered by his folks at home.

A feeling of emptiness engulfed him when it was time to return to the US. On his flight back, Ramu thought of his parents and wondered when he would see them again. He already longed for the home-cooked traditional meals, especially *puliyotharai* (tamarind rice), *paruppusuly* (beans cooked with lentils), hot *pongal* (steam-cooked rice and lentils), *sambar* and *rasam.* As the plane got ready to take off, Ramu thought of his old friends whom he missed a lot. Seated in the window seat, with a panoramic view of the Thirusoolam hillock, Ramu wondered when he would see all this again. Madras had a huge place in his heart and it was time to leave it behind again. This left him with a heavy heart.

Mylapore or Massachusetts... Arranged or Love Marriage?

The year was 1989. It was a very cold evening in December. Ramu was sitting on his dining chair, looking out of the window of his beautiful colonial village apartment and enjoying the snowfall. Chittamuru, his house-mate and a graduate student pursuing higher studies in the department of electrical and computer engineering at the university, handed him a thick envelope he had found in the mailbox.

From the appearance of the envelope, the stamps, and the hand-writing on it, Ramu knew it was from his father. From the thickness of the envelope, Ramu knew the letter would be brimming with several details from his mother, photocopies of horoscopes, and maybe even photographs of prospective brides. This was the pre-Skype and video-conferencing age. His father sent him such mails from time to time, urging Ramu to choose a girl for marriage.

Ramu's youngest brother, Anand, after completing his veterinary sciences degree in Madras, was pursuing his Ph.D. in molecular and cellular biology in the same university that Ramu studied in. Anand was studying the reproduction of cockroaches for his thesis while Ramu was working in the area of adsorption of polymers in confined geometries. Whenever both the brothers were free (invariably after midnight) and not arguing on issues ranging from the atom to the Zombie, the two of them enjoyed reading old letters from their parents and analysing them for hours. Both of them also enjoyed cooking, *ghoshti ganam* (group singing) and gossiping about their little town Nanganallur.

That night Ramu was alone. He opened the latest envelope from his father. This time his father had written at length. Ramu's father had urged him to step out of his *brahmacharya* (single) state and enter the *grahasta* phase (married). He had picked out several horoscopes (of prospective brides) from the monthly magazine *Sri Narasimhapriya* published by the Ahobila Mutt. The presiding *jeer* (head) of the mutt was his holiness Mukkur Azhagiyasingar, an exceptionally learned scholar. Mukkur Swami, as the *jeer* was known as, had embraced Ramu into the Vaishnava fold by performing the *samasranam* ritual.

Along with the letter, Ramu's father had enclosed a photocopy of his matrimonial advertisement from *Sri Narasimhapriya*. The advertisement detailed Ramu's personal details and other details such as educational qualification, place of work and salary. Ramu's father had also enclosed the responses received for the advertisement along with the details about the girl and her family.

The letter contained Ramu's father disappointment that despite receiving many responses, Karaikudi *josiyar* had found none of the horoscopes to match Ramu's. The eighty-year-old astrologer was gifted in reading horoscopes to the minutest detail. Ramu's father completely trusted the *josiyar* to find a good match for his son. He would not proceed with anything till the astrologer writes on the horoscope, "porutham seiyalam" ("matches, can be performed"). Ramu's mother always followed the more practical route and would say "anjukku moonu pazhuthilla" (three out of five is not bad) but not Ramu's father who would not agree to move an inch or even an a nanometre, unless he sees, "porutham seiyalam" on the horoscope. Ramu was the seventh in his family and the astrologer had always been consulted in the marriages of his older siblings.

Karaikudi *josiyar* was famous for ripping apart the horoscope and turning it into a horror-scope if he suspected that the parents were concealing vital details about their son or daughter, like a criminal lawyer tearing apart liars. The astrologer was very precise in predicting the fate of people based on their horoscopes, like a prospective boy would die in an accident in the next two years, a girl had been married earlier, or she would not be able to conceive.

The *jathagam* (horoscope) is drawn based on one's time of birth, geographic location of birth, and the position of planets at the time of birth and the year of the birth. The *panchangam* or the Hindu calendar is also consulted in preparing the horoscope.

It starts with this Sanskrit *slokam.*

Janani janma sowkyanam,

Varthani kula sampatham,

Padavem poorva punyanam,

Lickyathe janmapatrika.

This translates roughly as, "Birth is to live with pleasure and comfort; increasing the wealth of one's lineage; status/

position is the result of what has been earned by way of past good and thus is written the horoscope."

Following the *slokam,* the factors chosen to write the horoscope are written down (time of birth, place of birth, year, Hindu year and month, star at birth and gender). Two adjacent squares measuring 8 inch by 8 inch are drawn. One is used for *lagnam* and the other for *rasi.* The 8x8 inch square has four 2x2 inch squares inside. The location of the planets such as the sun, jupiter, saturn, raghu and ketu are jotted down in the smaller squares (also known as *gruha* or house) with respect to the time and the place of birth.

Other details (*lowkikam or worldly details*) such as the boy or girl's education, the father's position, and a few details about the brothers and sisters are also written down on a page. The borders of the horoscope paper are marked with *turmeric-kukmum*, as a symbolic indication of the beginning of auspicious things (*subham* or *mangalam*).

Ramu's mother visited the Navaneetha Krishnan Lakshminarasimha Swamy temple twice a day, once in the morning and once in the evening. The good Lord not only listened to your grievances and unloaded you of mental tension but also made sure that you know that you were not the only person coming to him with a variety of grievances. In those days there were no cellular phones or even enough land line telephones and despite this the community would come to know that Karaikudi Josiyar had a success rate of 100 % from the gossip circulated during the regular visit to the temple. So if one had to know what was happening in Nanganallur, a visit to the temple would suffice. Although Ramu's mother went to the temple as she believed the lord listened to her grievances and relieved her mental tension, she could hardly ignore the reputation of Karikudi Josiyar's prediction.

Her only grief was Ramu's marriage was not getting fixed. With her husband's insistence on Karaikudi *josiyar's* approval (which was hard to get), there was an inordinate delay in finding Ramu a perfect match.

Karaikudi Josiyar's predictions were invariably written in the horoscope and the information that was percolated through the wireless local loop of the Nanganallur community also confirmed that his predictions were "dead" right.

Ramu went through his father's letter in great detail. He paused to look out of the window to see the snow. "Arranged marriage," he sighed. His American friends often teased Ramu.

"How did you manage to grow up without girlfriends?"

"Are you serious when you say you have not have any physical relationship with a girl till now?"

"My first physical relationship with a girl was when I was thirteen and the girl was sixteen. We did it in my girlfriend's father's car."

"How is it possible to marry someone you do not know?"

Initially, Ramu's answers were largely self-righteous and serious in nature. At times, he would even reel out statistics on how there were fewer divorces in India. Over time, he realised that his friends were also concerned that Ramu was not living what they believed was a 'normal' life and that he was not willing to find his own life partner. They could not understand how Ramu can agree to marry someone without knowing each other's sexual compatibility, likes and dislikes and expectations.

While initially America gave him a huge culture shock, Ramu soon got used to what he saw – his friends' romantic dalliances, violent break-ups, reunion, and break-up again. Slowly he began to understand the nature of man-woman relationships in the US. Ramu curiously watched everything around him as a silent observer.

Ramu came up with an explanation for the phrase 'falling in love.' In one of his post-research group meetings, when the topic of Indian arranged marriages came up, Ramu put forth his theory to his colleagues and advisor who reacted as though he had dropped the bomb on Pearl Harbour. Ramu equated his theory on love to the first law of thermodynamics, which states that the energy of the universe is constant.

Ramu used the word 'bombing,' as his theory was too simple and it shook the foundations of what his colleagues called 'love.' Ramu called it the necessity-convenience-love theory or NCL theory.

The Indian society, in theory and to a considerable extent in practice too, is well-known for certain quantum selection rules on man-woman relationships with its emphasis on developing one's clan. The western and American model, on the other hand, believes in the need for a physical relationship and the hormones to be in sync, similar to the way one craves for food through the secretion of acid in the stomach. When there is a build-up of hydrochloric acid in the stomach, we start looking for food. The food has to be edible, tasty, and presentable and should not cause side-effects to the body. It has to be easily available and accessible.

Many of Ramu's American friends said they broke up with their girlfriends since 'long distance relationships' do not work. But Ramu did not think that distance had any nothing to do with 'love.' In theory, love is said to have conquered the space-time relationship. For instance, in the Ramayana, Sita's love for Rama and Rama's love for Sita was enhanced by their separation, in space and time. But necessity and convenience have everything to do with 'love,' believed Ramu. Once necessity (hormonal factors) and convenience (ease of accessibility) are met, the next thing that follows is 'love.'

But Ramu's theory was at conflict with what he had learnt in his Tamil and Sanskrit classes. Kamban, Kalidasa and other poets had expressed, so beautifully, that love was a spontaneous feeling emanating from both man and woman, at the first instance. Ramu was also reminded of Kamban's *Ramayanam* which stated *annalum nokkinaan avalum nokkinal* (Rama and Sita fell in love with each other at first sight). But having seen so many instances of 'love-at-first-sight,' Ramu was convinced that this NCL theory was largely valid in the US.

Ramu bravely presented his theory to his American friends, after one of the research group meetings. They were shocked and had no defence against his findings. His thesis on this subject passed without much ado!

Later, Ramu expanded his NCL theory without disrupting the second law of thermodynamics, which said that a system, when left to itself without intervention, would progress towards more and more disorder in the universe. Ramu proudly explained that the Indian marriage system was designed in such a manner that it did not violate the second law of thermodynamics.

Therefore, Ramu decided he would follow only the Indian tradition and marry according to the established customs of his family. Also, Ramu did not have the confidence to even talk to a girl. He, in fact, always avoided any situation that required interacting with the members of the opposite sex. Life in Nanganallur had not prepared him in these matters although he could have picked a leaf from the llife Seshadri or Suresh or Ramesh on the dark steps of Modern School.

Although Ramu rejected the American way of romance and marriage, he also did not truly believe arranged marriages worked. He did not like the sound of a matrimonial ad announcing 'Vadagalai, Koundinya gothram, Uthirattaadhi, 28, Ph.D., US, looking for a post-graduate, musically inclined, family-oriented, linguistically talented with appropriate culinary expertise. Bride's party may please reply with horoscope and photo."

It was early evening in November 1989. The CNN news channel was discussing the world's population. The population index, displayed at a corner of the television screen, reported that there were close to one billion people in India. Around 50 per cent of them were male, so, Ramu thought, he was left only with 500 million women to choose from, assuming he was going to marry an Indian girl. Among them, easily 400 million would not qualify - as 100 million would be below the legal marriageable age, while 300 million would have been married already. That left him 100 million to choose from.

Among these, Ramu would only consider Tamil speaking girls as he did not want to use western terms of endearment such as 'honey' and 'dear.' That left Ramu with a smaller population of 5 million to choose from. Now, since Ramu's father was particular about the caste and the sub-caste, the number drastically reduced to 25,000. Ramu then remembered that the advertisement in the *Narasimhapriya* had a very important condition that the bride would have to be a post-graduate. This left him with just 2,500 (Ramu's sharp mind did all the calculations in no time!).

Ramu was really nervous and as he went through the advertisement his father had placed in *Narasimhapriya* again. Of the 2,500 potential horoscopes, Ramu was certain that about 2,000 or more would get rejected on some criterion such as "not-musically inclined", "not-family oriented" or the other. That left just 500 proposals in the hands of the astrologer. He pictured Kaaraikudi *josiyar* sitting before a picture of lord Hanuman and rejecting most of the horoscopes, one after the other.

Ramu remembered that the astrologer had rejected all the 109 horoscopes his father had once meticulously picked for his elder brother. Of the next lot of 85 horoscopes, the *josiyar* had approved only one. Given the *josiyar's* history, Ramu was sure he was going to be left with just two or three women to choose from.

Ramu was saddened by his plight. He had not even made a beginning and with all the conditions imposed by his family, he had little freedom to choose. This would be true of the bride too. Arranged marriages didn't believe in making a choice. It worked more on the principle of elimination. Ramu wrote a letter to his father as to why arranged marriages would not work. Ramu's father ignored his letter and went about his way and didn't even bother to reply to Ramu's letter.

At this rate, Ramu thought he would have to remain single for life, merely observing life around him. A frustrated Ramu planned to visit India at the beginning of December, not quite trusting his father's process of match-making. He packed his things and flew down from Massachusetts, hoping for a miracle to unfold during his month long visit.

The miracle did happen. Within ten days of his landing an elderly woman visited their house with a marriage proposal as the horoscope of Ramu matched with that of her daughter Janaki. There were just two days left before the beginning of the Tamil month Margazhi, during which time marriage proposals are not discussed. Ramu's parents agreed to visit the house of the woman at Choolaimedu the next day. After the visit and with the Ramu and Janaki agreeing to marry each other, the ball was set to roll. In just a month's time, Ramu's parents arranged his marriage. Things proceeded at a hectic speed – first the wedding, followed by arranging the passport and visa for Janaki.

Janaki joined graduate school in Amherst. Years went by. Soon, the two of them were busy working towards completing their Ph.D. Ramu. Janaki and Ramu often spent hours together discussing their future. What did Ramu and Janaki want for themselves?

Both of them loved the comforts of a hassle-free life in the US. This was the land of dreams and they both had a meaningful professional life here. But they often missed the small touches of India, more specifically Madras. Every telephone call back home would fill them with nostalgia and longing. But it also saddened them that Madras was still lagging behind in terms of convenience and comfort. Ramu, a student from a lower middle class family, had come up in life to enjoy the comforts of the US. What could Janaki and Ramu do with their education to turn around their hometown?

Ramu's heart often flip-flopped between Madras and Massachusetts. Repeated visits to Madras drained Ramu emotionally and convinced him that he and his wife belonged there. Ramu was left with a strong urge to complete his education and return home to enjoy the simple pleasures it had to offer. Although sometimes he secretly wished he could transport all the comforts of the US to Madras for his relatives and friends to appreciate and enjoy. But convincing his folks about the goodness of the US seemed a Herculean task.

There were times when Ramu experienced a hollowness living in the US. At the same time, he was not sure if returning to India would be professionally rewarding. It wasn't an easy decision to make. Janaki was more than happy to get back home. But Ramu seemed to lack the courage and conviction to give it all up and move back home.

One fine day, Ramu wrote down the pros and cons of living in the US. Ramu felt that life the US was predictable and monotonous, bordering on boredom. On the flip side, things like power cuts, water shortage and bad roads were unheard of in the US. The quality of drinking water was monitored and controlled. Cable television ran 24 hours a day and telephone conversations were free from disruptions. Restaurants were open round the clock and in case of an emergency, the ambulance, fire service or the police arrived in no time. Everything was in place. The Americans were an innovative lot. The American system of education encouraged creativity in every field, be it arts, music, sports or science.

In India, people did not appear to value one's time. When someone asked you to come and visit them the next day, and you did visit them, you would be asked to come again another day. It appeared as though one would be tested enough for their commitment before they received any thing significant. But in the US, people valued one's time and kept up their promises and commitments. Ramu appreciated this quality a lot.

Ramu liked the American commitment and predictability. At the same time liked the balance between order and disorder, predictability and unpredictability that he could get in his home country. Especially the unpredictability aspect of India was more interesting. Every political rally, every poster on public walls, every cow and dog on the street, every power cut or instance of water shortage and every bad road in India taught him to value what he had and thank god for every little blessing. It taught him not to take anything for granted. Ramu was not sure if he was cut out to enjoy the comforts, order and discipline of life in the US at the expense of the home-brewed environment and value system.

He thought that his personal choice, only if his partner would agree was a combination of availability and deprivation that would make him ponder a lot and enjoy what was available. Janaki liked the life in US. Her Ph.D. in molecular and cellular biology was attracting several job offers with an annual salary of $80,000 plus perks. But she offered her unconditional support to Ramu if he chose to return home.

Ramu remembered telling Janaki's parents that he would eventually return to India. He also remembered the promise he had given to the American Embassy in Madras, when his F1 visa application had been rejected the first time around, that he would return home after his studies. For long, he had been procrastinating. Janaki was pregnant and they were expecting their boy within the next three months. It was time to make the big move, decided Ramu. The day after Janaki defended her Ph.D. thesis, Ramu and Janaki booked their return ticket to Chennai via San Francisco and Singapore. A week later, they boarded the flight back home. Ramu could not wait to see if the Thirusoolam hillock was still there where he had last seen it!

Glossary

Aavani	One of the 12 months of the Tamil calendar (August to September)
Aaranyam	Forest
Adyar	A small river through which the rainwater flows from the south-west part of Madras into the Bay of Bengal
Akkaranthaha	Words ending with the sound A
Akka	Elder sister
Aththan	Husband
Avittam	One of the 27 stars each representing a day in a month
Ayyappan	A Hindu deity
Bhajanai	Group singing of devotional songs
Brahmopadesam	The ceremony of teaching the *Gayatri mantra* wherein a young boy is initiated into the *Brahmacharya* phase of life, in which he studies the Vedas. This involves the *Upanayanam* ceremony wherein the boy is made to wear a sacred thread.
Chitragupta	Account-keeper of good and bad *karma*
Elai	Leaf
Engengo	All unknown places

Ennai	Myself/me
Ghanam	Singing
Ghoshti	Group
Gilli thanda	A game played with a one-foot wooden stick of one-inch thickness that is used to hit a four-inch long wooden stick of one-inch thickness.
Goli	A game in which glass marbles are directed into a small hole on the ground, similar to golf, using the finger as a projectile
Hari	Vishnu, the god who sustains life
Ilavasam	Free
Indru	Today
Intha	This
Iyengar	A sub-caste of Tamil Brahmins
Iyer	Another sub-caste of Tamil Brahmins
Gundu	Fat (in Tamil Language)
Kaalani	Footwear
Kaadhu	Ear
Kalyanam	Marriage
Karumaariamman	Hindu village goddess
Khaandam	Part
Kolu	A thematic arrangement of dolls over several steps on an inclined plane. This happens during the Navaratri festival

	celebrated during October-November every year.
Kondu-pogudhu	Takes away/ drags
Kurangu	Monkey
Maama	Married Tamil Brahmin male
Maami	Married Tamil Brahmin female
Maapillai	Bridegroom/son-in-law
Manamagal	Bride
Manapandal	The stage where the wedding rituals take place.
Mangalyam	The chain (gold or beaded) that married women wear
Marumagal	Daughter-in-law
Mayakkam	Drowsiness
Mothagam	A sweet eat
Nama	Name
Pandal	Stage
Pon	Girl
Poojai or Pooja	A method of worship
Pulinkaha	Male
Sannidhi	A special enclosure for a particular idol
Shabdham	The phonetic sound of a syllable
Sankeerthanam	Music
Slokam	A verse written in praise of god
Sundal	Boiled and spiced lentil
Thittam	Plan

Thozhi	Girl friend
Tiffin	A light snack
Valaikaappu	Baby shower ceremony
Vedanta Desikar	A saint born in Thoopul, near Kanchipuram. He is one of the major spiritual luminaries and intellectual gurus (guides) of those who practise Vaishanavism.
Vishnu sahasranamam	The 1,000 (Sahasra) names (namam) of lord Vishnu
Vaasi	Resident